The Red Runs Deep

by
WolfBear

Here's to life!
WolfBear

PublishAmerica
Baltimore

First printing

ISBN: 1-4137-5895-9
PUBLISHED BY PUBLISHAMERICA, LLLP
www.publishamerica.com
Baltimore

Printed in the United States of America

Table of Contents

Chapter 1: In the Beginning...

The fire made long shadows on the cardboard walls around it. The fire cracked and sparked, a life of its own, giving warmth to the Spring night. It danced in response to the Medicine Man's reverent chants. The surroundings were meager. A Sik-si-kau mother lay on a single blanket, her tattered dress her only covering. Beside her, in the center of the tiny space, was a well-contained fire, patiently tended, emphasizing the sacred moment at hand. The Medicine Man, One Feather Dances, fervently vacillated between gratitude and request as his words turned skyward. The young mother, obviously caught in distressed childbirth, lay near the fire circle, soaked with her own sweat and blood. An older woman, Grey Otter, sat near her head, a wet cloth frequently touching the fevered body as it writhed in an attempt to release the life within her. The flame rose and ebbed as if responding to the young woman's pain.

"She has lost a lot of blood. Napi-quan has left her scarred and labor is hard. We must pray that she delivers this child soon or they both may die." One Feather Dances paused in his prayers as he spoke to Grey Otter in traditional tongue. She seemed lost in her prayers, concern and pain etched on her own face.

Grey Otter had known One Feather Dances for more than two decades. She trusted his abilities to meet the needs of her daughter and arriving grandchild. One Feather Dances had once been held hostage to the addiction of alcohol, as many of the Reservation was.

He had fought hard to reclaim his power from White Man's Poison. It had not been easy. One Feather Dances was slight built, his frame resembling the single feather for which he was named. As he danced, his shadow shifted to resemble a feather floating to the earth. Grey Otter knew that Flower Beneath the Stone had his Spirit supporting hers through the ordeal.

"The child has the strength to live. They have both survived so much already. The time is close for the arrival. I must get more rags to contain the bleeding. Sit with them for a moment," she responded, also in traditional tongue. Grey Otter rose and slipped out of the room. In the other room, behind the blanket that served as the door, Grey Otter paused and sighed deeply. The pain she was forced to watch as her own flesh writhed in the pains of childbirth, hurt her more than any pain her own body had ever known.

One Feather Dances squatted beside Flower Beneath the Stone and began his quiet, chanting prayers again, his hands moving the length of her body, never touching, sprinkling sacred herbs and the medicine they contained. In response, Flower Beneath the Stone screamed, pushed, screamed again. One more push and a tiny life emerged from her body. The cry was weak, but grew stronger as One Feather Dances raised the baby girl from the dust. Indians appeared from beyond the walls and Grey Otter rushed over and wrapped the newborn in a rag, handing her to her mother. She then set about controlling the bleeding as Flower Beneath the Stone cried tears of happiness and relief. The infant, now quiet, raised her eyes to meet her mother's. "Her eyes are smiling. Through all of this she still has a smile for her mother." Flower Beneath the Stone, though exhausted, was obviously pleased.

"So shall her name be Laughing Star. She comes to this world, burning bright in the night, bringing smiles and laughter to those around her. You are both lucky." One Feather Dances barely finished his words before Flower Beneath the Stone was asleep, her infant nestled sleeping in her arms. The cardboard walls danced with the shadows of the firelight as half a dozen other Natives milled about, congratulating one another on the arrival of the newest member.

One Feather Dances raised his baritone chants for Flower Beneath the Stone and her newborn child. They would need much protection and strength to find the guidance they needed to navigate the darkness brought by Napi-quan, the white man who had won Flower Beneath the Stone in a poker game. She had escaped to her people to give birth to this child. But One Feather Dances feared the white man would search for her and come to take her and her children.

Grey Otter finished cleaning up and lifted the tiny infant. "Hello, Granddaughter. Welcome to this world. You have much to learn, much to overcome. But your Spirit is strong and the Ancestors are with you. Your journey shall become a lesson for all those willing to hear. You are destined for great things."

Just then, two dark skinned toddlers, twins, stepped from the darkness. "Look children, your sister has arrived." As Grey Otter spoke, she held the baby in one arm and extended the other to speak with her hands, sign language. The boy, Little Red Feather, squealed and babbled a combination of English and Native Tongue. His Sister, Silent Stone Beside the Water, seemed to grunt but her hands responded. She had been Deaf since birth, honored by her People as a chosen child. The family had taken the ancient Indian sign language and combined it with the little American Sign Language they could access. It made for a crude language, but fluent for the immediate family and Silent Stone communicated clearly. For those unfamiliar with the language, someone was always nearby to give voice to her hands.

The toddlers, about two years old, touched their new sister gently, exploring her lighter skin. The difference in skin color obviously perplexed Silent Stone, who raised her eyes to Grandmother. "She is of Napi-quan, a halfbreed. It is not important, she is still your sister and a member of this Tribe and family." These first two were full bloods, conceived just before Flower Beneath the Stone had been taken into her slavery life. This new infant was the result of the ravage the white man brought into Flower Beneath the Stone's young life.

Laughing Star was a tribute to the perseverance of her mother. Although the slave owner could rape, beat and break her body, Flower Beneath the Stone knew he could never break her Spirit. This child was evidence of her will to go on and Spirit's approval.

Looking down to the infant, Grey Otter said with both her words and her hands, "Laughing Star, meet your brother and sister. This is Little Red Feather and Silent Stone Beside the Water." Laughing Star smiled in her sleep.

As Grey Otter bent to place the infant in her mother's arms, she met the eyes of Flower Beneath the Stone. "Her life will be hard," the older woman spoke in traditional tongue. "She will not be welcome in the white world and even here, there will be challenges. Her Spirit is strong. She will survive."

"I know, Grey Otter, but what can I do? She *is* beautiful."

"Yes, she is."

Chapter 2: Bridging Worlds...

Grey Otter's words were low as she spoke with the Elder, "The children are finally relaxing. Flower Beneath the Stone's body is finally healing. The infant has grown strong in her first few weeks. What are we going to do to protect them? They are ours and soon he will come for them. His work of the Demons is no life for anyone, let alone our own."

"There is little we can do if he comes. For now, they have the protection of our silence."

Grey Otter was obviously not pleased by the response, but she knew that the Elder had spoken and arguing was useless. She extended her gratitude and left quietly. As she entered the fire circle, she was greeted by the children, "Tell us a story, Grandmother, please!" They begged. She smiled and lifted a smaller child to her arms as she sat on a log within the circle. The children, about six or seven of them, clambered to sit near enough to hear. Though they were not all her grandchildren by blood, she was an elder for them all and thus related. She loved them each with all her heart and they returned her affection. She reflected for a moment as she began her story...

> Once a grandson came to an old Indian Grandfather and spoke with anger about schoolmates who had done him an injustice. Grandfather sat

with his grandson and listened. Then he explained, "I, too, have felt great hatred for those who have taken so much with no respect and little sorrow for what they have done. But hate wears on your body and Spirit. It beats you down. It is like drinking poison yourself and wishing your enemy would die. I understand your struggles, Grandson."

The young boy looked at his grandfather, taking comfort in his words. Grandfather continued. "It is as if within me live two wolves. One is good and does no harm. He lives in harmony and takes no offense when no offense is intended. He only fights when it is right and only in the right way."

"The other wolf, he is full of anger! The littlest thing sets him into an enraged fit. He fights all, all the time, for no reason. With anger and hate so great, he cannot think clearly. It is hard to live with both these wolves within me, for they both work hard to dominate my Spirit."

His grandson looked intently into his eyes, "Which one wins, Grandfather?"

Grandfather returned the gaze, looking deeply into his grandson's eyes and said solemnly, "The one I feed."

The children sat for a few moments, quietly, as if digesting what they had just heard. Then, like a shot, they exploded into childhood chatter and scampered off, sending back words of love and gratitude to Grey Otter. She smiled and waved as they headed off to do what children do.

"I've come for what's mine!" The man's voice was impatient and threatening as he spoke to Grey Otter outside the encampment. Little happened out there that word did not provide warning for. When the Indian boys had come to tell her of the white man's arrival, Grey Otter and three large Indian men had met him outside the walls of the encampment. She didn't want his feet to touch sacred ground. She also wanted to give Flower Beneath the Stone freedom for as long as possible. Grey Otter wished for days when warriors would have defended and fought this lone man off. But those days were gone. The Tribe that was left struggled to maintain their own existence and could not afford to take on such a challenge. Grey Otter also believed there were those among them who practiced the ancient Devil arts, like this white man. How else could a young Indian woman have been lost in a poker game? How else could he have come again and been so confident she was there? Grey Otter chose not to understand it.

"You have come a long way to claim a lowly Indian woman." The Winter Wind had released its icy grip, but the smell of cold still lingered in the air. Spring was waiting on the edges.

"I've come for the halfbreed, too. Is it a boy?"

"No, she is a beautiful baby girl."

"Damn! Well, tell the bitch to pack up. We leave in an hour." He turned away without giving her a chance to respond. Grey Otter walked back to the shelter, her mind somewhere else as her feet led her forward to begin packing a small bag. It had been almost a year. There were moments, when she watched the children playing and laughing, that she thought they might be safe, that he might never find his way back into their lives. She had been wrong. Deep inside, she had known it would happen. But it still brought tears to her eyes. In the satchel at her hands, she laid four medicine bundles, one for each of her precious Spirits. As she packed their meager belongings and dried meat, she chanted a prayer of protection under her breath.

Grey Otter knew well the destruction of white man. She had watched over the last several years the tumult between the white and red worlds. Her family had always been politically active. It had cost most of them their lives and not one person noticed. It was just another dead Indian. She looked up to meet the eyes of Silent Stone.

"Yes, my child. He has come to take you back. I'm sorry." Her words and hands conveyed the information slowly, painfully.

Tears welling in her eyes, Silent Stone fell into the arms of her grandmother. Together they cried, one last time.

Chapter 3: Laying the Foundation…

Flower Beneath the Stone splashed water on her face, gently rubbing her bruised eye. Napi-quan had wasted no time in delivering retribution for her escape. Her ribs, back, legs and face bore evidence of his anger from the night before. Fortunately, the children were all safe in bed before his drunken tirade began. She alone had felt his rage. Flower cursed him silently as she heard his footsteps approach the bathroom door.

"'Bout time you got up, you lazy bitch. Fix me some breakfast."

"I need to feed the children." She spoke softly, not wanting her words to be mistaken for a challenge.

He spat the response, "Those little prairie niggers and that halfbreed can wait! You'll cook my breakfast first!"

As if to emphasize his authority, he slapped Flower across the face with the back of his hand. The insignia ring on his finger stung her already bruised cheek. Dutifully, she walked to the kitchen, trying to prepare his breakfast before the baby awoke. Her body froze as she heard the shriek of pain from Laughing Star. She rushed to the bedroom, fearing what she might find. Red Feather also came running to his mother's side, eyes wide with fear. Silent Stone came a few paces behind. She had followed the urgency of her brother, but was unaware of the circumstances since she could not hear her sister's cry.

"Shut the brat up, bitch!"

She lifted the 10-month-old infant from the drawer of dingy blankets that served as a crib. Flower noted the reddened hand print across the baby's face.

"She sleeps too much. I decided she needed to be awake now. You know, young pussy brings a good price on poker night." He made the statement with a greedy glint in his eye.

Flower shivered. She knew that to ensure her children's survival she would always need to be close at hand. She pulled them to her as he left the room.

As if on cue, Lori appeared from the other room. This was his wife. She was not happy about Flower and even less so about the children. She sneered as she walked past them. "I see your live-in whore and her leeches have arrived. I can't believe you went after them!" She leaned up and kissed him.

He kissed her back and smacked her ass, then turned to the children and their mother. "Breakfast 'bout done? I need a shower. Don't let it get cold." He grunted as he walked toward the bathroom with Lori. "Oh, and John's here tonight. Make sure there's plenty o' beer."

Flower knew nothing good would happen when the two men were together. If things were bad when he drank alone, they were worse when he had company. Shaking her head, she hustled the children to the kitchen.

Without a high chair or playpen, there was no other place for the infant so Flower placed the baby in a sling across her back. Flower liked having Star so close. It reminded her of home where things were different. With the gentle movement and the sound of her mother's heartbeat nearby, Star was soon back to sleep. The twins played quietly at their mother's feet while breakfast finished cooking. He and Lori ate first and then the children. If there was enough, Flower would eat, as well. Most mornings she did without.

By the time breakfast was done and she had cleaned up, he had left for work. Or at least that was the premise. She knew there were days he never made it to the machine shop. Those were bad days because his drinking started early and the more he drank, the meaner he became. Lori was off somewhere. She said little as she left. She never talked directly to Flower, not that she had anything to say that Flower wanted to hear. Anytime Lori referred to her it was as "the

whore," "the bitch," or "your injun cunt." Though they were never directed at her, those words stung Flower to the heart. She tried hard to remember who she really was. But the longer she was away from her People and the more the darkness overcame her, the harder it was to reject the negative messages of worthlessness and pain. She knew, too, it was hard for the children. So, each night, as she tucked them in, she sang the loving songs of The People, of Creator and gratitude. She told them the old stories, using the Native tongue so they could truly understand the lessons. She used her hands and pictures so Silent Stone missed nothing. Although Laughing Star was so young, she still laughed and cooed with her siblings and clapped and patted the rhythms.

These happy moments sustained Flower during the daily turmoil. In moments of beatings, whether physical or verbal, she would visit those few precious moments with her children and cling to that reality as the darkness around her tried to feed on her Spirit. The work of the Devil around her had to be countered with strong forces of goodness. She knew of little stronger than the love between a mother and her children.

Chapter 4: His Foundations...

It was Friday night, poker night. Flower Beneath the Stone knew as the evening sun began its descent that nothing good would happen. Weekends were always dangerous times, but this Sunday also brought the full moon. Her memories fell back to her People, where such an occasion was a tribal celebration. Here she knew it would be treacherous.

The two older children played on the kitchen floor at her feet as she finished dinner preparations. The baby slept quietly in a corner. Little Red Feather met his mother's eyes as they listened to his footsteps ascend the stairs. The child's eyes were filled with fear and it broke Flower's heart not to be able to reassure him that all would be well.

The slamming door startled Laughing Star who began to cry. His thunderous hand reached the infant before Flower could snatch her up. The quick backhand sent the baby rolling and the cries turned to shrieks. He lifted the infant for a moment before tossing her to the wall. The infant fell silent. His anger then fell to Flower who was well within his reach. He punched her hard in the mouth and stormed, "How many times do I have to tell you to shut that halfbreed up? You're lucky I don't just kill you all."

As he stomped out of the kitchen, Flower regained herself enough to turn to her infant daughter. Red Feather and Silent Stone were already touching their baby sister in an attempt to revive her. As the

baby began to stir, Flower knew she would have to keep Star quiet or the next round might be fatal. She scooped up the infant, checking over the tiny body that was shaking from fear and pain. Star whimpered. Flower began to softly sing a traditional song in Native tongue, trying to sooth the baby's thoughts.

Overall, Star had sustained a significant bump and bruise on the side of her head from the wall and a nasty welt from the back of his hand, but she appeared otherwise okay. Cradled in her mother's arms, Star quietly cried, seeming to understand that sound might be followed by more pain. Her tear-filled eyes looked into her mother's, begging for comfort. Flower gazed back into the dark pools and offered a silent prayer that this tiny one would survive the ordeals that lay ahead. She thought back to the ominous words of Grey Otter regarding the hardship this child would endure. She took comfort in knowing that Grey Otter had also commented on the strength Star had that would allow her to survive.

Flower was jolted back to reality by the sizzle of the stove. She didn't dare burn dinner, so she sat Red Feather down and placed the baby gently in his lap. Star could sit pretty well alone, so all her brother had to offer was support and comfort. He and Silent Stone, knowing the importance of stillness, played simple finger games with the baby to keep her mind off the pain and entertain themselves.

As Flower tended to dinner, he entered the kitchen door. "I have people coming tonight. It's poker night. Don't put the brats to bed. We'll be needing them." He sneered. "You, too."

He grabbed a plate and piled it with the beans and potatoes. "Where's the meat?"

"It's in the oven. I'll get it out."

"Hurry up. I'm hungry."

Lori walked in the door just as Flower raised the ham from the oven. As if on cue, Red Feather and Silent Stone picked up the baby and left the room. "Glad to see you made it home sober on payday," Lori said to him.

"Poker night. Guys are comin' here."

"So, you spent our money on booze for the boys?"

"Some. They'll be bringin' the payoffs for the shipment they moved this week. Don't worry!"

"Rent is due. Electric's gonna get shut off if we don't pay this week."

"Yeah, yeah, yeah. I'll give you what you need."

"Don't forget that your whore clan costs us more for food and stuff, too!"

"The baby will need goat's milk," Flower quietly interjected, hoping not to incite anger, but knowing that what she had brought with them from home would not last more than a couple more feedings. Star was eating solid food, but still required three bottles of goat's milk to stay healthy. Flower had already diluted the present supply.

"She can drink powdered milk from now on. It was good enough for my mom, it's sure as hell good enough for her." Lori didn't really say this to Flower, but the point was made.

Flower made up a meager plate for her and the children and hustled off to the back bedroom. This room was the closest thing they had to sanctuary. She had fashioned beds for the children. The drawer fashioned with blankets as a crib was tucked against the corner, two of the walls of the room serving as a kind of fortress. The back of the dresser was at the foot of the crib and the single mattress the twins shared to the only other side. Flower, herself, slept on the floor in the bedroll she had brought from home. The only other thing in the room, besides the satchel Grey Otter had packed, was the white lamb's rug that was given to Star by the Tribe the day she was born. It was here Flower would talk with her children, gathering around the rug allowing it to serve as the center of their 'fire circle.'

Seated around the circle, the children were encouraged to ask and question, wonder and learn. Flower took great joy as she watched the twins, hands and mouths flying, challenging and teaching each other. Silent Stone had found this to be the only place she could communicate freely and clearly. Often, her questions were about the workings of this strange place and the contrast between here and Home. These were difficult questions, posed by bright youngsters who did not yet possess the awareness necessary for the answers to what seemed simple questions.

"Why is he always angry?" "Why did he hurt Laughing Star?" "Did he bring us here only to hurt us?" "Doesn't anyone care that he hurts us?" "I hate him!"

Flower tried hard to answer their questions honestly, but in ways they could understand. At almost 4 years old, the twins had spent many hours listening to the stories of the Ancients told by their mother and Grandmother. Flower often used these stories to remind the children what they really needed to learn. Often she spoke in Native tongue, always supported with the signs needed for Silent Stone.

"Remember the story of the two wolves within? There is the wolf who is gentle and good, who works for the good of Spirit and all creation. Then there is the wolf who fights everyone, all the time, for no reason. Do you remember the story and which wolf finally wins? Which wolf gets his way inside us?"

"The one I feed." Red Feather recited.

"Good. And what does that mean?" Flower prompted.

"The wolf that gets the most for dinner?" Silent Stone offered, hands raised in question.

"In a way. In this story, it's not about feeding the wolves' tummies. It's about feeding their Spirit. What kind of Spirit does the wolf who is gentle have?"

"A gentle one," Silent Stone signed.

"Yes. And the one who fights. What kind of Spirit does he have?"

"A fighty one," Red Feather stated with words and hands.

"That's right. Here in this place, we see fighty Spirits because what they have been given and what they do is all about fighting and hurting. That's why things happen here that are so hard and hurtful. It's important, though, that we continue to do what we have to do to keep our Spirits gentle. That's why we must find good ways to meet the bad things that happen."

"But how, Mama, when he hurts Star so badly and makes her cry? All I want to do is hurt him back!" Red Feather pounded his little fist into the opposite palm.

"I know, honey. We have to try to love him. Maybe that way he can learn how he should really treat people."

"That won't work!" Silent Stone finished her sentence by mimicking her brother, fist to palm.

"It doesn't seem very likely, does it? But we must try." Flower's words fell to no one for the children were off in their own silent conversation, signing back and forth about how best to escape back home. She understood. She had successfully escaped once. She could do it again.

As Flower cleaned up the dishes and kitchen, the men began to arrive. Each took their turn to leer at her and the children who played in the corner. She did her best to ignore their hot breath as they got close behind her.

"Maybe you'll be mine tonight, squaw!"

"Wait till you see what I got for you. You'll be whoopin' those Indian hollers for more!"

"I'm feelin' lucky tonight! Gonna get me some prairie nigger pussy!"

"Hey, looky here. Baby squaw!"

"Oh, yeah. Baby pussy. Ain't nothin' sweeter!"

"I dunno. This boy look like he might be pretty sweet, too!"

"Yeah, but watch out for the little freak. She can't do nothin' but squawk and she can't follow no directions worth shit!"

Flower worked hard to tune out the conversation. It was as if she and the children were nothing more than meat in a butcher shop window. She found it hard not to take it in and feel the dirtiness they tried to force on her. She knew it would be a long night.

Done with the kitchen, she began moving the children to the back room. As she lifted the baby, she felt a sharp smack to her backside.

"Where you takin' 'em? I told you it was poker night. You need to keep these brats right here. Bring 'em to me when I tell you. Don't be in nobody's way and do as you're told. Better remind 'em of the rules, especially the little deaf-mute. No tears. No noise. No tell. Break the rules, I break you."

He took off his belt as he finished, landing a half-hearted blow to Red Feather's back. The boy jumped, but made no sound.

"I need to change the baby," Flower stated.

"Don't bother. That diaper won't be on for that long." He sneered as he walked to the other room. Flower followed with the children.

Just inside the doorway from the kitchen was another large room. This room had a double bed that served as his and Lori's bed. Flower sat the children on the bed.

The room was large enough for a card table with six chairs. Just beyond the large room was a carpeted room with a couch and television. The bathroom was next to that and the back room, the one Flower and the children shared, was next to that. The doorways for the living room, bathroom and back room all entered the large room, making it the center. This is where the men gathered, seating themselves, beer in hand, around the table.

"Okay, boys. Pay up. Whacha got for me this week? Gave you each enough to bring me $500 and have some left over for yourselves, cash or snorted. Where is it?"

"We all got it right here, Chuck." The tall man, John, spoke quietly.

"Yeah, and I'm gonna win some of it and a little pussy back myself tonight!" Lenny, Chuck's brother, was always a little too eager. *Not bright*, Flower thought to herself, *but eager.*

"Yeah, talk is cheap. Just pay up and then we'll get on with the game."

Each man placed a neat wad on the table. They milled around with cigarettes in their hands chatting until Chuck had counted it all.

"It's all here. Let's get started." Chuck lifted his head in the direction of the living room. "Lori, you gonna come watch and make sure your pussy don't end up on the table?" The men laughed.

"You got your whore and her little bastard clan, you should have plenty to keep your drunk asses happy. I'm watchin' t.v."

"That's only four and there's six of us. Seems you might come in handy." The blonde with dirty hands ventured. He was new to the table. Flower had not seen him before.

"Shut up, Curly, or I'll have to come in there and cut your cock off for kicks!" Lori obviously was well-acquainted with Curly. The men laughed as the game got under way.

21

Star screamed in pain. Flower had to bite her lip to stay the tears. Red Feather looked at his mother, face white. She looked at him and shook her head.

Chuck was angry now. "I told you to shut up, bitch!" Barely moving the bottle from inside her, he flipped Star over and began to smack her bottom. Confused, she cried and screamed, filled with fear and pain. It seemed to only anger him more as he moved her to the floor, removing his belt, he began to beat her. As darkness overcame her, Star stopped crying and her body went limp. As his rage subsided, Chuck turned to Flower.

"Get her up and ready. My cock hasn't even tasted her yet."

Flower's legs felt like lead as she moved to her baby, beaten to silence the second time today. As she bent to lift the silent form, she felt the belt on her back, butt and legs. She used her body to cover and protect the still unconscious baby as she thought of that Sacred Place that no one could tarnish. She let the blows fall until his tirade was done. Then, haltingly from her own pain, Flower carried the baby to the bathroom and began to rouse her. She used cool water on the welts and bruises, both Star's and her own. She could hear that they had begun their abuse with Red Feather. She shuddered, praying he would be spared the anger. Her heart screamed within her. She was powerless to protect her own children, destined to watch them die, feeling their pain beyond her own. She vowed she would find a way to release them.

"Hurry up. My pecker is lonely!" Chuck yelled to her from the large room.

Laughing Star was awake now, but not at all recovered from the ordeal. Flower Beneath the Stone tried to think of a way to spare her. Obviously, her thinking slowed her too much for Chuck's liking. He was at the bathroom door and reached out, taking the baby with one hand and smacking Flower in the head with the other.

"I told you I was done waiting. She's awake. That's all I need."

He took the infant to the bed, dropping his pants to the floor. The older children were huddled on the floor in the far corner, themselves naked and tear-stained. Flower went to them and knelt beside them,

shielding their eyes from the scene with her body as she turned her back to what was happening.

"Watch boys, this is how you break a whore in good."

He put his penis to Star's lips. "Okay, you halfbreed bitch, just lick it like a lollipop. You and Daddy are gonna play a game. You do exactly what I tell you and you're gonna like it. You break the rules and I'm gonna whip you with my belt again. Uh uh... no tears. Didn't your mama tell you? No tears, no noise, no tell. So, open wide and lick the lollipop."

Star was confused. She didn't understand what to do. She didn't like what was being pressed against her face. She opened her mouth because she didn't know what else to do. Maybe she would have cried out. Maybe she would have had something to say. She was never sure. It was in her mouth, choking her before she knew what to do. And he kept pushing it deeper and deeper into her throat. She tried to cry, but nothing came out. Tears came down her cheeks. Then he took it out. And she started to cry.

"No tears!" SMACK. The sting on her face stopped all sound from her mouth.

Before she could breath, Star felt his fingers near her vagina. Nothing could have prepared her for the tearing pain as he entered her with his penis. She could do nothing but scream. Still insider her, Chuck smacked her face. Hysterically, Star screamed and sobbed as Chuck thrust and smacked her simultaneously. The men behind them were enjoying the show and whooped and hollered their approval. Star closed her eyes tight and wished herself away, far away. The sounds around her faded. Everything went dark and quiet.

Chapter 5: Where Demons Tread...

The sun woke Flower that Sunday morning. She had spent Saturday comforting hurting children, trying desperately to keep them quiet and well-tended. She was concerned that Laughing Star may have sustained significant injuries but here, in white man's world, there was no Medicine Man. Flower did the best she could with the meager supplies in the satchel and made sure they were each comfortable. Chuck had slept most of Saturday and Lori seldom spoke to Flower or the children, so Saturday had passed gently. But today... today there would be trouble. Tonight it was the full moon. Unlike Home, this was not a pleasant experience. Flower shuddered as she thought of the dark cloaks and candles that would mark the ritual here. The Demon's ritual.

Shaking her head to clear the thoughts, she got up. The children were all sleeping so she walked quietly to the kitchen and began making breakfast. She heard Chuck stir and rise, listening as his footsteps led him to the bathroom. But then, he was taking too long. Her concern filled her as she stepped to the doorway. The back room door, where the children were sleeping was ajar. She knew she had closed it. Then she heard what she feared, the irregular cry of Silent Stone. Flower froze, unsure what to do. She knew if she appeared at the door he might take pleasure in making the child suffer more as Flower watched. She felt she was betraying the child by standing, doing nothing.

As these thoughts of conflict rose within her, he emerged from the room. "You know how it is in the morning. Man wakes up hard, he wants a little relief. Found it." He laughed at himself. Then stumbled back into bed.

"Breakfast ready soon? Why don't you bring it to me and Lori here in bed? And make it quick!"

Flower ducked back into the kitchen and prepared a tray to take to the bed. Her thoughts raced so fast she could not keep up. In her haste, she dropped the sugar bowl. She went for the broom to clean up the mess. When she returned, broom in hand, he was standing over the mess.

"This ain't good. Such a waste. Come over here. I said get over here now. Get down on your knees."

"But there's glass there from the sugar bowl."

"Shoulda thoughta that before you broke it, huh? Now kneel there and suck my cock. Put the goddamn broom down and hold my balls. That's it... ahhhh"

Flower did as he directed, feeling the glass dig into her knees as he pushed and pulled her head in his ecstasy. He took forever to cum.

"Now get this mess cleaned up and get us fresh breakfast. That shit's cold. Feed it to the brats." He left the room.

Flower stood up, gently brushing away the glass from her knees. The cuts were superficial. She finished sweeping the mess, cleaned up her legs and went back to cooking breakfast. When done, she took the tray to Chuck and Lori. Lori was already in the bathroom. Flower set down the tray then returned to the kitchen, reheated the first breakfast and took it to the children.

Silent Stone sat on the edge of the mattress, tears still falling silently, Red Feather with his arm around her. Laughing Star lay still sleeping. Flower set the tray down on the rug and went to the twins. She took Silent Stone into her arms and allowed the child to sob into her shoulder. Red Feather stared off, eyes angry. Flower touched his arm gently. She could think of nothing more to do and nothing to say.

Evening approached. Chuck tossed black cloth and clothesline onto the bed in the large room. "That's what you and the brats are to wear tonight. Nothing else. Just tie it at the waist. You know how." Then he walked into the kitchen.

Flower took the children to the back room. She undressed each one, noting the bruises and cuts that had not yet healed. She touched each of them with Sacred Oil, praying for their safety and protection. Then she took one of the smaller pieces of cloth, folded it in half and, using a kitchen knife, cut a hole in the crease. She put this over Silent Stone's head, tying it at the waste with a piece of the clothesline. She repeated the procedure for Red Feather and herself. For Laughing Star she altered it slightly, using diaper pins at the sides to hold on a diaper and prevent the use of the clothesline. She refused to risk the infant getting tangled in the rope. There were enough dangers tonight. Those that could be avoided would. And so they sat, waiting.

Flower took advantage of the time together. She softly sang a loving song that talked about the Directions, the Elements and all of Creation and the love that flowed through and among them all. It was to remind them that they were all connected, all One in Spirit and so were all loved and lovable. The children sang and signed the words they knew and rocked to the rhythm the Native language provided. It was a peaceful moment filled with love and light. Flower knew this was good.

The footsteps in the hallway brought back the foreboding feelings. Chuck stood at the doorway. "Hurry up. Can't be late. Get in the car. All of you in the back seat."

They drove silently for quite sometime, Chuck and Lori in the front, Flower and the children in the back. The terrain changed. The urban, inner city gave way to grass, fence and trees. Although it was late at night, the full moon lit the sky. The car slowed and pulled back into a lane. A large barn lay in front of the headlights, a small house to the left. Chuck barked directions and Flower got the children out of the car with her. They walked to the barn. The night was cold. The children, wearing so little, shivered. Flower held the baby close, hoping to keep her warm. She looked at her children in the

moonlight. They still bore evidence of Friday's abuse. She couldn't bare to think what lay ahead. As they walked behind the barn, the circle came into view. Dark cloaked people, some hooded, gathered around a fire at the center. Chuck came to Flower and took the baby. Flower watched as the infant's cloth was removed, diaper and all. Her tiny nakedness was stark against the black clothes around her.

Flower pulled the twins close to her. They stood in the circle, Flower tried hard not to focus on what happened before her. Laughing Star, her sweet innocent baby, was being given into service to Satan himself. Sexual acts from those within the circle were to seal the baby's fate. A cup of blood would be passed. Flower had showed the twins how to fake the sip, allowing no blood to touch their lips.

Quietly, throughout the night, she countered their incantations, calling upon the Spirits of The Ancestors and Creation, the cardinal Directions and all that is Good, Right and Just. She called upon all she knew and all she could know to imbibe within this child all that was needed to survive the unsurvivable. As evil taunted around her, Flower lifted the Spirit of Laughing Star so that she might rise and thrive, live to be an example of love incarnate, as a beacon to a world lost in Darkness. Flower vowed her own commitment to ensure whatever was necessary for this to come to fruition. As the demonic ritual grew to a close, Flower once again became aware of her surroundings and saw a limp Laughing Star on the ground at the center, blood leaking from her vaginal and anal openings. Her tiny chest heaved in labored breaths, validating that life still lingered in the broken body.

As the others left the circle, Flower, followed by Red Feather and Silent Stone, went to the infant. Gently, Flower wrapped the baby in the cloth tossed to the ground and held her to her. Star was cold to touch, but breathing. Chuck walked up to Flower. Before he could speak she said, "You almost killed her."

"She's still alive. She's my kid. They all know they can't kill her. I rule here. Don't give me lip or I'll make it so you can never talk again! And don't you EVER look me in the eye again! Take her over to Marge. She'll fix her up."

Flower lowered her gaze. The twins gripped the sides of their mother's cloak and walked with her as she carried the baby over to the house. Marge was another of Chuck's harem. She had his son, Charlie, who was 5 years old. Marge had some kind of medical background and was always referred to as "The Nurse." She had patched Flower up in the past. Her methods usually included narcotics to "help with the pain." That translated into sleeping until the pain wore off. It was Marge who had ensured Flower's addiction before the escape. The Tribe had helped Flower get clean. Flower had no intention of allowing Marge to trap her again. She knew she needed to be careful.

Marge met Flower on the porch and reached out for Star. "I'll carry her myself," Flower stated, careful not to look the woman in the eye. Marge complied and turned to enter the house, Flower and the children behind her.

Flower laid the baby on the couch in the front room. Marge came in with warm water, a warm baby bottle and a bag of medical paraphernalia.

"What's that?" Flower pointed to the baby bottle.

"Warm milk to help her sleep."

Flower was sure there was more in the bottle than milk, but any further challenge and Marge had the power to call down the wrath or deliver her own. She had to let it go. Marge packed off the babies bleeding orifices, used a cool rag on her head and talked gently to Star until she roused a bit. Then she gave the baby the bottle and watched with satisfaction as Star's breathing patterns indicated sleep.

"You don't look so good either," she stated, turning to Flower. "Do you need anything?"

Flower's memory shot quickly to the drugs and addiction of the past. "No, thank you. I'll be fine."

"What about the other children?"

"They are doing fine, thank you."

Marge looked in their direction, shook her head and stood up. "Well, if you change your mind, let me know. You can sit here for a little while. The festivities will continue downstairs. I'm sure you will be invited shortly."

Flower knew that meant she and the twins would soon be raped and battered. Her thoughts betrayed her as she wondered, *Has Creator forgotten us and left us at the hands of Evil?* She shook off the negative thoughts even as she heard heavy footsteps approaching. She kissed each of the children and quietly reminded them of the rules, simultaneously praying for the survival of their Spirits.

Chapter 6: New life???

It had been six months since their return to Hell. Flower could no longer hide the life within her that she had brought from home. As her pregnancy became more evident, she feared for her life and that of her unborn child. She told no one that the father was one of the Tribe, the love she had hoped would save her from this life. In the end, his fear of Napi-quan prevented him from even considering defending her. This child was all she had left. But if Chuck figured out the child wasn't his it could be fatal.

As winter approached, she could wear heavier clothes to cover the obvious. The clothes Lori brought from the thrift store were always too big and heavy. It was a blessing for Flower and the children since the flat was often cold. Now the blessing was doubled. Yet Flower was unsure of exactly when to expect the newborn's arrival. If it was too soon, Chuck would figure it out. She prayed that she had just a little longer.

As she gazed at her children, all three sleeping in the early morning, she could see the cost this life of demons had on them. They were thin and scarred. Each of those little bodies had already withstood what Warriors should never know. How could she bring another life into this hell? But what was the alternative? Creator had a plan. She was only a small part of the big picture. Her physical existence had no way to comprehend the greater good. She accepted that all things happen as they should for a reason. Lifting her smoke

in gratitude and prayer, her eyes caught sight of a spider in the upper corner of the room, hanging in the web she had spun. Flower thought of the size of the spider, so much smaller than she herself. She remembered back to the stories of Spider the Weaver who weaves life and aided Creator in the making of all that is. Such a small creature. So very great in the Big Picture, the gifts of the tiny bug used as part of a greater whole. Flower took comfort in the lesson given, knowing she too had gifts that were a part of the greater Good. She smiled as she looked up and saw the light that glowed around Laughing Star. Ahhh, a special Child. Flower accepted the sign that Star would survive.

Flower lay on her bedroll, alone in the dark. It was Time. The baby was coming. She was unsure of what to do. She might be able to sneak from the house and go somewhere to give birth. But where? And what of the children should Chuck and Lori discover her absence? She lifted her Silent Voice to the Ancestors and asked for their help and guidance. She looked at the clock. It was 12:30 AM. She closed her eyes to the next contraction.

Chuck entered the room at 9:00 AM. "Where's my breakfast, bitch?"

He stopped short, looking down at the bedroll where Flower and the newborn lay. "What the hell? Why didn't you tell me you were pregnant, ya whore? Lori!"

Lori was already at the door. "You fucked her yesterday, couldn't you tell she was pregnant?"

"I was a little stoned, I guess. So, what is it, a boy or a girl?"

"It's a little boy," Flower spoke softly.

"'Bout time!" Chuck seemed proud and grinned. "Okay, Lori. That means you need to go get breakfast ready. And make sure there's enough for her. Gotta help my boy be strong!"

Flower was unsure how long it would take for Chuck to realize Mica was not his, but she was not about to tell him now. She lay quietly as the children came to visit. Red Feather had brought his sisters over

to their mother to greet their new brother. The children were excited, though Silent Stone seemed concerned.

"Mama, his skin is like mine, not Laughing Star. How can he belong to Napi Quan?" she signed.

"All will be well, little one. We are all one, remember? And we are all family. Color doesn't matter. Come here, say hello to Mi-ca. Isn't he beautiful?"

Laughing Star had come to accept that this was how life worked. She couldn't remember anything different in her two years of life, so how could she believe anything more existed? The contrast of life around her seemed quite normal. Mama talked of Light and love, of being connected and Spirit that moved within and around. She smiled, talked softly, gave warm hugs and cried with her heart when Star or the others were hurting. But Daddy... well he was a scary monster that only held sharp words and painful touch. He had rules with grave consequences and games that she could never win that left only scars and pain. He worked hard to break the Spirit of Star, Red Feather, Silent Stone, Mama, and now Mi-ca. Mama worked to mend and bind the Spirit, to keep the Light of hope alive. Star didn't understand all of this as such, but she knew well the difference between the love she felt from Mama and the darkness Daddy brought. She didn't think about these things as thoughts, but as pictures and feelings, as visions and knowings. She lived moment by moment, sometimes in the soft warmness of Mama and sometimes in the drugged haze of Daddy. Conflict outside that she struggled to resolve within.

And so, as she heard the footsteps approaching in the darkness of night, she rose to one hand in her crib. Quietly, he lifted her and laid her on the rug in the middle of the room, a few feet from where Mama pretended to sleep. Star gagged on the overwhelming smell of alcohol and sleepily fidgeted. Menacingly, he motioned for silence. Star lay quiet and obedient, understanding that anything else meant the sharp retribution that could lead to severe pain. He undressed her, removing first the woolen sleeper and then the moist diaper. For a moment he just knelt there, gazing at her body, her legs slightly apart.

she might, Star couldn't help the cries that came from within her. He didn't seem to notice and kept his hand tightly clamped over her nose and mouth. She couldn't breath and couldn't stop the tears. Darkness started to come over her just as he came and removed his hand. He held her, almost upside down, while he caught his breath. Then with one move he stood her in the shower. "Stand right there!" he ordered. Star didn't move.

He disappeared for a moment then returned with a small hose and bottle. "Bend over." He inserted a plastic end of the hose to her anus and squeezed warm liquid inside. When done there, he had her shift so he could do the same to her vagina. It burned a little, but really helped make Star feel better.

"Now I want you to wash Daddy." He handed her the soap and helped her soap her hands and guided them to his shaft, balls and anus. They were about finished when the door opened and Lori stood in the doorway.

"You horny bastard, you never get enough!"

"Hey, don't wanna waste resources, now do we. Got sweet baby cunt that needs to learn what to do, who better to teach her than the great Dargon?"

"Yeah, yeah, toot your own horn. I could show her a thing or two, as well."

"Well, you can have your turn when I'm done. Sloppy seconds, you know."

"Not tonight, I have a headache."

"Okay. Go get the kid some ice cream. Put some of the leftover stash in it. She'll sleep it off and think it was all a dream."

"Alright, but then you need to come to bed."

"Now who's horny?"

"Don't flatter yourself. I'm cold." Lori smiled as she said it and left the room.

"Okay, my baby slut. We're done here. Let's go get some ice cream with sleepy stuff. That's what Daddy's special bitch gets!"

Star withstood the abuse and torture, flirting occasionally with death. Mama taught her and the others how to go inside, how to find that sacred place where no one could hurt you. Star would go there often during abuse, shutting out the things that were too horrible to bear, too painful to withstand. She would just float away.

Inside, things were beautiful. There were others to play with and the world was green and sunny. It was always safe and warm. Bear and Eagle came often to Star's Sacred Place with words she didn't always understand, but always with comfort and warmth. Short of Mama's arms, Star preferred to be inside than anywhere else.

Chapter 7: And Then There Was One...

Rapes, beatings, near death experiences, ritual abuse... it all continued for Flower Beneath the Stone and her children. She had tried to conceive an escape plan, but each one had been foiled by a move to a new flat or an unexpected change in how things were done.

Chuck considered his drug and gun trafficking quite a success. He worked for The Organization as the top dog in the area, the Dargon. Those that knew him feared him. Those that weren't smart enough to fear him usually ended up dead. It all meant he had a reputation to protect and he was proud to do just that. Sometimes it meant he had to relocate his clan to stay ahead of trouble, but only until he found the weak link and put the law in his pocket. He now had free reign of the city and could do, as far as he and his superiors were concerned, whatever needed to be done.

He avoided getting too comfortable in routine since he had seen that come as a downfall for other leaders within The Organization. Communication kept his people moving like a well-oiled machine. And the money rolled in. He had enough after paying his suppliers for his personal needs; ponies and women. He managed a personal stash. This was what he used to keep his home whores addicted and predictable. The Indians he had acquired came with names, but he didn't like them. After all, they were part of his world now. They needed names fit for the white world. He was nice, since he needed them to answer to them, he asked them what they wanted. The

woman chose Rose. She called the older twins Matty and Patty. His baby wench she called Alissa. And the baby boy was called Micah. He had balked a little over the baby's name until he figured out that it wasn't his. Then it didn't matter what she called it. He left it alone—for now.

Sometimes, to maintain order, people had to be made an example. The need had arisen again and he needed all the right people to see it. He woke Rose and had her dress the children to go out into the bitter night. It was about 2 AM.

He sent them out to the car as he got coats for himself and Lori. They drove for a short time and stopped on an overpass. He ordered everyone out of the car. They stood on a highway bridge overlooking another highway that passed below. Truck traffic moved beside and below, the only real traffic at this early hour.

As they approached the berm, another group was huddled there. It was Lenny's clan, his three children Amy, Deanna, and John, and his wife, Eileen. As Flower and the children came closer to the clan, Flower noticed that Eileen's hands were bound and her face was bruised and tear-stained. Eileen's children stood with wide-eyed fear. The children were just about the same age as Flower's, John just a few days older than Star. The brisk air was an eerie cold.

Chuck looked at Eileen. "You know better than to try to leave. You belong here with us. This is the only place for you. But you keep tryin' to leave! The last time you tried we told you it was your last chance. Didn't you believe us?"

Eileen just looked at him, resigned and pale. Chuck grabbed her bound hands, walked her to the guardrail, looked at her one more time, then pushed her. There was no sound until a thud of the truck that hit her below. By the time the sound reached their ears, both clans had dispersed back to their vehicles to disappear. Flower didn't need to see the newspaper article the next day to know Eileen's fate.

Flower knew she was present for Eileen's sentencing for a purpose. Chuck must be aware of her thoughts. She must have left clues. Perhaps the extra rations she was stashing in the satchel. Perhaps her

more frequent refusal of the nighttime tea she knew was laced with narcotics. Regardless, Flower knew she must act soon if she was to succeed at all. She looked at her sleeping children, the four gifts in her life. It was for them she must escape. Tomorrow.

Chuck had left for work and Lori had gone out to where ever. Flower finished cleaning up the kitchen from breakfast and began last minute preparations. Mi-ca was just 17 months old and would require the most care along the way. Keeping him quiet and happy would be the biggest challenge. 3-year-old Star was an easy child to entertain. The 5-year-old twins were great with their littler siblings. But it would be a long journey Home and Flower knew she would have to take a different route, initially, to throw Chuck off her trail. There were great risks, but none greater than the risk of staying.

Flower briefed the children. She spent extra time with the twins, making sure through question and answers that they understood what was ahead. They seemed to understand. Flower was packing the last of their things, had the baby in the sling on the bed, ready to place on her back when Chuck unexpectedly walked in the door. She turned to face him. He pulled a gun from the holster at his belt he always carried. She wheeled around, fearing he would shoot at the children. She made it to the doorway of their room and looked on the faces of her three older children as she heard the shot. She felt the heat in her back as the world went fuzzy, watery, and black.

"No!" screamed Red Feather as he rushed to his mother. He pulled her onto his tiny lap. Silent Stone and Star stepped toward them, but Red Feather stopped them with a raised hand. "Stay away!" he said to them. Then to Mama, "Please don't leave us, Mama. NO! NO! NO!" His hysterical cries continued as Star slinked under her lambskin rug, trying to hide from the horror in front of her. She watched as Mama's blood covered Red Feather and he rocked her.

"Stupid bitch! She knew better. Got what she deserved. All right you brats. This mess is all your fault. Now you're gonna help clean it up. Quit your blubberin'. We have to clean this mess up. Tell the

freak to get the baby outta that thing and unpack that bag. Go into the bathroom and get the dirty towels and start cleaning up this mess."

Alissa didn't move under her rug. She prayed to be invisible, to go with Mama away from this place. She watched as Matty interpreted to Patty what she needed to do with Micah. When Matty got up to get the towels he silently went to the rug and took her hand. "Do this with respect. No matter what, you gotta think about good things about Mama while we do this. Don't let him make you forget that, okay?"

Alissa nodded, not sure what it meant. As they walked to the bathroom and began the formidable task of cleaning up the blood, she played the warm and happy memories of Mama. She remembered the stories, the songs, the games, the time. It hurt, but it also made her feel a little better.

Chuck had put Mama in several plastic trash bags. It was late. Lori had come home to the mess, had a fit and finished cleaning what the children couldn't. Patty did her best to care for Micah, but he was often inconsolable. It was obvious he understood the least. He had never been away from his mother's side. He didn't comprehend she would never be there again.

Chuck loaded them all into the car, with Mama in the trunk. They drove to a cemetery not far from the flat. Chuck drove around, looking for something. Having found it, he got out of the car, went to the trunk and took out shovels and the bagged body. As the children got out of the car, another car approached. It was John.

"Geez, Chuck. Did you have to shoot her?"

"Ah, hell. It's just another dead Indian. Ain't nobody even gonna miss her."

"Yeah. I guess. So, we just gonna put her here in the cemetery?"

"This is a new grave. We just dig down a little ways, put the body on top of the one that's already in there, put the dirt back and nobody'll ever know it's here."

"Seems a little sacrilegious. I mean, I wouldn't want no dirty injun cunt buried on top o' me!"

40

"Dead don't know no different. Okay you little niggers. Grab a shovel and start diggin' right here." Chuck pointed to a mound of dirt that was clearly recently moved. Matty moved in the direction of the shovels, talking to Patty who fell in behind him as he walked. "Remember the crossing over words Mama taught us? We need to use those now," he signed to both his sisters. "Don't say them out loud. Say them inside, in your heart where Mama is now."

Alissa was too little for the shovels so she held Micah on her lap nearby. She repeated the words Mama had taught them when their pet mouse had died. Chuck had set traps in the house and the little mouse had been caught but not killed. The children had brought it to Mama who tried to tend the tiny creature. Despite her efforts, the mouse had died. She took the opportunity to talk to the kids about *Crossing Over*, how it was not an end as some people thought, but merely a change in form. She taught them the Ancients' words that would help their new friend move on in his journey from this place to the next.

The children understood very well the portal to the Cross Over. Each had spent time at the doorstep, brought to near death by the abuse and torture they withstood. Matty had felt the power of the words and had worked with Mama to memorize those words. He taught them to his sisters in re-enactments of the ceremony they used for their pet mouse. All the children were glad for that experience now as they used those words to comfort their own loss and feel a part of their mother's journey.

Matty and John were the ones who finished the hole. Chuck dumped Mama's body out of the bags and into the hole. Matty couldn't bring himself to shovel dirt back into the hole. Chuck struck the boy from behind as he stood staring into the hole at his mother.

"You wanna go in there with her? Get diggin'!"

Matty resumed the task, halfheartedly. Patty helped a little. Alissa sat giving cheerios from her pocket to the baby to keep him quiet. None of them was sure what life would look like now without Mama.

That night, as Star began to fall asleep, she saw a White Wolf approach her. Familiar with Bear and Eagle in her Sacred Place, Star was unafraid and introduced herself to this new guide.

"I know who you are, Laughing Star," said Wolf. "I am Mama. I have come to be with you, to guide you and love you from here. You have done well with this Sacred Place. Is it okay for me to stay here?"

"Yes, Mama, please. Stay with me here, White Wolf. Can you hold me? Rock me? Make the hurt inside stop?"

"I cannot make the pain stop, my child. But I can ease the pain. As you grow I am here. I will make sure you don't forget to whom you belong."

"Who is that?"

"You are Mama's daughter, Creator's child. This is the truth that shall live within you. And you will survive!"

"Hold me while I sleep. I am afraid."

"Well you should be, Beloved."

Lori stood over Alissa's naked body with a belt. "Let's see if you can get it right this time. I'm your mommy now. Don't ever even think about that other bitch. You're mine now. Who am I?"

She raised the belt as Alissa looked up, welts on her face, arms, back and legs from the beating she had already endured. "Mommy," she whispered as she cowered back, fearing another blow.

"Good girl." Lori lowered the belt "Let's go get some ice cream."

The house was quiet now. Matty and Patty lived somewhere else. Alissa and Micah were alone with Lori and Chuck. She saw her siblings at the rituals and some of the parties and celebrations. That meant the only time they had together was during abuse or drug induced highs. Matty tried to remind them about the good things Mama had taught them using sign from across the room. He had had several of his fingers broken for his efforts, but still he tried.

Alissa tried hard to remember all the things Matty talked about. She talked to White Wolf often, feeling the maternal presence, clinging to the comfort it brought. But it got harder to resist the outside messages. Lori tolerated no mention or insinuation that Alissa had ever had another mother. It was as if Lori alone had born and raised this child. Alissa knew better, most of the time.

Lori all but ignored Micah. She tended to his basic needs, but nothing more. Alissa would spend as much time as she could with her baby brother, playing with him, hugging him, telling him about Mama. If Lori overheard such things, she would whip Alissa with a belt or broomstick. That meant Alissa had to become more discrete in her conversation with Micah.

Being ignored seemed a good thing. Micah suffered very little of the daily abuse. Even at demon's time, short of being passed around for orgy enjoyment, Micah seemed to be ignored. Alissa didn't understand it and was sometimes jealous. Nonetheless, she knew Mama would be pleased for Micah's good fortune, so she remained content as well.

Alissa's experience was far from similar. Despite Lori's claim to love her, she continued to turn Alissa over to Chuck and The Organization to do with as they desired. Parties, rituals and celebrations occurred every weekend and the rape and the abuse seemed to support their words that Alissa was nothing more than a whore, a slave to them and their ways, one of them and destined only to please each of them.

During the week, she was forced to succumb to Daddy's games. She could never win and the retribution seemed to likewise support the evil she was told. This created a great conflict for Alissa, so she set out to protect herself as best she could. She locked a part of herself away for safekeeping, the part of her that Mama loved and nurtured, that White Wolf could guard and protect. That was the part that was innocent, sweet, and untouched. Alissa knew that part needed to be locked away until the time came when it might be safe again. She didn't know *when* that would be, but she knew it *would* be.

In the outside world, Alissa learned well the rules. No noise, no tears, no tell. Halfbreeds are not really people. Never look a white man in the eye. Suffering builds character, so shut up. Ask no questions. Do what you're told—every time. You cry, you die. Smile and everything will be fine. Pain is in your imagination. They thrive on your fear and your pain—never let it show!

By the age of 4, Alissa had learned how to turn off pain. All she had to do was to put it in the palm of her right hand and squeeze. She

WOLFBEAR

could hold it there indefinitely. If she ever felt control was slipping, like she might show something she shouldn't, she merely had to clench her left fist. If none of that worked, close your eyes and disappear to that Sacred Place.

She could sometimes look directly into the eyes of the one on top of her and see nothing, show nothing. There were times it unnerved her perpetrator. It always seemed to annoy them, for they fed on her fear. It meant the beatings got worse and the retribution and punishment was more severe, but somehow Alissa felt it was the only way she could win. After all, wasn't winning what it was all about?

This full moon ritual was different. Alissa had been instructed to wear a hooded cloak. She was not yet 5, had completed the rite of passage at 3 years old, and was not yet old enough for the rite of passage at 5. But the hooded cloak was for a ritual leader. She was confused.

As Chuck, known here as Dargon, led her to the center of the circle at his side, the horror and comprehension struck her. On the altar at the center of the circle, prostrate and tethered, lay Matty. An outside altar, just to the left, held Patty. Alissa stopped dead in her tracks. Chuck lifted her arm. "Keep moving. Tonight we prove you are one of us."

It was obvious Matty was drugged. He was barely conscious. His body bore evidence that he had been raped and beaten, the blood still fresh. Alissa could not see Patty clearly, but knew by the sounds her sister made that she was not as drugged as their brother, but in severe pain. Her heart cried out to comfort them. When she looked up she met Dargon's cold stare and knew her life depended on her behavior this night.

The incantations began. These rituals were the opportunity for the dogma of traditional Christianity to be inverted and the Powers of Darkness were called upon to do the evil bidding of the clan that staked its claim here. This clan had become a community and subdued its members by fear and pain and offered power and euphoria as the rewards. It was a clan that partook in a myriad of criminal activity including drugs, gambling, sex, guns, slavery, child

porn, and stolen goods. Their guilt bound them together and their silence kept them safe. Alissa, an unwilling participant in all their endeavors, hated them all. As she stood over her brother, she felt Dargon's hand over hers. He placed a large knife in her hands, his cupping hers. In a swift blow, he threw the blade into the boy's chest, Alissa's hands on the handle. Blood sprayed out, in Alissa's face and down the altar. "You have killed him! You are one of us!"

Inside, Alissa screamed and cried, "No!"

But outside she could do nothing but what she was told. Dargon moved her to the second altar. Patty looked Alissa in the eye, begging for comprehension. Alissa could offer none. As the blade pierced Patty's heart, a scream Alissa had never heard before echoed. She realized it was the Spirit of her sister, released from its pain. Covered in the blood of her siblings, Alissa could do nothing but accept the death of a part of her within, a part that would seek to join her siblings as they Crossed Over. Silently, the young child mourned. And went inside to her Sacred Place.

It was Halloween. 5-year-old Alissa was home alone watching Micah. They were playing on the floor when Lori came in. She was unusually happy and talked to Micah with a lilt in her voice Alissa had never heard before. Lori knelt beside the toddler and picked him up with a bag over her arm. She took him over to the bed and began to dress him. To Alissa's amazement, Lori was dressing Micah in a ghost costume.

The anger welled within Alissa. Did Lori have a costume for her, too? The attention Lori gave to Micah was unusual but all Alissa could think of was what he was getting that she was not. It wasn't fair! Alissa sat on the bed beside them, quietly, knowing she was to be seen and not heard. Asking questions could be fatal.

Chuck came in shortly and, ignoring Alissa, took Micah from Lori. The two adults then walked out the door with the little one, leaving Alissa alone. She didn't know what to do with herself. Not that this was the first time they had left her, but it was always with Micah. Now she found herself completely alone. She was confused.

As if on cue, the door opened and John walked into the room. She had been instructed to call him "Uncle John," though he was no blood relation. Alissa's jealousy quickly changed to fear. Uncle John's games were worse than Daddy's. He was rougher and meaner and he liked to make Alissa and Micah cry. Alissa still didn't understand what was going on.

"Your mom and dad went out to a party tonight. You and I are gonna have our own party."

"No. I don't want to. I want to go with them."

"I think you forgot a few things, bitch." John picked her up and moved to a corner in the living room, lifting the lid to the wooden toy box, dropped her in. He sat on the top and Alissa felt the heat and fear. The toy box was kept empty for just such an occasion. Alissa hated the box. It was small and cramped. It got hot fast and John sat on it to prevent her from opening the lid even a little.

"When you remember the rules, you can come out. But you have a hell of a lot of apologizing to do."

There was no use in fighting it. Alissa could either sweat it out as the panic within her began to grow or she could tell him what he wanted to hear and get on with it. It wasn't like the bad stuff wasn't going to happen one way or another. And if Chuck came home and found out what she had done, there would be a whipping for sure.

"I'm sorry. I'm ready now."

"Good." He opened the lid and she stepped out. "Strip for me. I'm gonna heat your ass up for that little shenanigan and then we can get on with the party."

Alissa began removing her clothes. First her shirt and then her pants, panties and socks. She stood naked before his leering eye.

"Now bend over and grab those ankles. You count each swing and tell me thank you."

SMACK!

"One. Thank you.

"Thank you, SIR. Start again. You got ten coming and don't miss nothin' or we start over."

SMACK!

"One. Thank you, sir."

SMACK!

"Two. Thank you, sir."

SMACK!

By the time she got to 5 she couldn't feel anything anymore. She knew better than to allow the tears to fall. She robotically finished, "Ten. Thank you."

"It's thank you, SIR. Start over!"

SMACK!

She forgot what to say. She just froze. He waited. Hearing nothing, he spun her around to face him.

"You really asking for it tonight, huh? Well, I'm the one to give it to you."

He grabbed her by the back of the hair and half-dragged half-carried her to the bathroom. He shoved her headfirst into the toilet. She managed to gulp air before her head was submerged. He held her there for a minute.

"Not enough for ya, huh? Well let me piss in it to make it better."

He didn't move her head as he whizzed in the water.

"When you've had enough, we'll try the whipping again. I'll have to find somethin' a little heavier this time so you don't forget how it goes."

Lungs screaming for air, Alissa flailed her arms.

"Had enough, huh?" He looked her in the eye.

She looked away and nodded.

Still holding the back of her hair, he stepped her into the shower. The warm water felt good. He let go and disappeared. Alissa stood up straight and ran her fingers over the bump on her head where she had hit it when he shoved her face into the commode. John was suddenly next to her, naked, with a short strap of leather.

"Bend over. Figure this'll help you remember who's the boss. Count!"

SMACK!

Wet leather on wet butt and legs stung. "Ow! One. Thank you, sir."

Lifting her by her hair, he smacked her across the face with the strap. "I don't want to hear, ow, just count and tell me how much you want to thank me! Start again!"

SMACK!

This time to the upper leg. "One. Thank you, sir."

SMACK!

"Two. Thank you, sir."

SMACK!

Alissa kept her head through to ten this time, not wanting it to get any worse. She was plenty sore from the welts of the belt and strap by the time he was done.

"Let's move to the living room for the party!" John turned off the water and reached for a towel. He dried her off, smacking her ass as he sent her out the door.

Alissa knew it would be a long night. She wished she had been allowed to go with Micah. He got a costume and everything.

As Uncle John's games began, Alissa closed her eyes and went to her Sacred Place.

It was morning. Alissa had ended up on the floor in her room on her lambskin rug, naked, bruised and hurting. But it was over. She went to the bathroom and found her pussy and ass were bleeding. She used two tampons and shoved them into the openings, as Daddy had taught her, so as not to stain anything. She walked out into the living room. Micah was on the couch.

She walked over to him. Horror took her breath away. The little body was dead still, dead still because he was dead. His face and fingers had a bluish tint. His eyes were wide open, the blank stare of death. Alissa just stood there, staring. She didn't hear him come in.

His angry voice boomed, "You want to be next?" In one motion, he swung something in his hand and severed Micah's head from his body. Alissa couldn't even scream. Who would hear her? She was alone.

Chapter 8. Family Dynamics...

It was late. Mommy sat in the living room. Alissa could hear the television and an occasional cough. Daddy wasn't home yet. Alissa knew that tomorrow would be the first day of kindergarten. She was excited, but afraid, too. Here at home she knew the rules, knew what to expect and how to behave. That didn't mean she didn't break those rules, sometimes on purpose, but at least she knew what to expect. New places meant new rules. And what happened when she broke those rules? Daddy had already said if there was any trouble at school there would be more at home. That didn't sound very good, as if he expected there to be trouble. It was hard for Alissa to sleep, her mind racing. She laid as still as she could, wishing herself to sleep. Suddenly, she heard a loud noise. It was the front door to the apartment. Daddy was stumbling in.

Voices, far from quiet, began to echo through the hall. They got louder as Mommy and Daddy fought over this and that. It was not unusual. The fighting was a pretty constant thing at night. When Alissa could sleep, it often was loud enough to wake her. She could even here the blows that fell, the smacking sound of his hand on Mommy's body. Bruises seemed to be the family colors.

There was a crash, stomping, slapping, a thump, then silence. Alissa sat up, concerned. Silence was unusual when both her parents were in the house. She slipped from her bed and crept to the door. Peering out, she saw only a light down the hall from the living room.

Quietly, for she knew the consequences if she was caught, she tiptoed down to the light. The scene startled her.

Mommy was standing over him, table lamp still in her hand. Daddy was on the floor, not moving. Alissa could see he was breathing, a trickle of blood from the side of his head. He lay very still.

Lori's eyes glanced to her, "He almost killed me. We have to get outta here before he comes to. Go get dressed. Hurry!"

Alissa knew by the tone of voice that it was urgent she follow the directions quickly. She darted back to her room. Finding the new clothes laid out for her first day of school, she decided this was not the occasion to wear those. She shoved those in the old satchel along with her bear and blanket. The bear had been with her since she could remember. It was a Pooh bear, made from a yellow towel and hand stitched and embroidered. Alissa couldn't remember exactly where he had come from, but she also couldn't remember a time she didn't have him. She slept with him every night. Pooh was special and had to go with her. She dressed in her old jeans and a flannel shirt, careful to button it the right way as Mommy liked. She was just finishing when she heard her mom's voice from the other room.

"Hurry, honey. Grab what you can. We gotta go."

Alissa looked over her shoulder at the room, wishing the tattered white rug on the floor could fit in the satchel, but knew better. That was all she had, except for a few more clothes. Somehow she knew things were changing. Her heart whispered goodbye to her rug and she hurried to the front room. Lori was waiting.

"We'll have to take the bus. We'll go to Grandma's for tonight and think about what comes next in the morning. She knows how he is, she raised him." Touching Alissa's cheek gently, she then took the little girl's hand in hers and headed down the stairs and out into the night.

Alissa was familiar with the buses in the big city. It was how she and her mom went grocery shopping and visiting the family. Grandma, Dad's mom, was one of Alissa's favorite people in the world. She was short and round with a soft, deep voice that was never

raised in anger. If Grandma was around there was always plenty of hugs and good food. That helped to counter the other things that happened there.

There were eight cousins from Dad's brothers and sisters who got to hang out together at Grandma's. Alissa was the youngest and, many said, the grandparents' favorite. Grandma and Grandpa were the loving people in Alissa's world. Country-western musicians, they played in the local bars at night every weekend. During the week, Grandpa worked for the railroad as an engineer. In Alissa's imagination it seemed a good balance. Grandpa blew the train horn during the week and then cut the rug with his guitar on the weekends. Music all the time.

Alissa loved the music. Grandpa played lead guitar while Grandma played bass fiddle. Grandma had to stand on a crate to reach the full length of the massive instrument, but together they were very good and never lacked weekend work. Uncle Dale, the youngest of the brothers, played steel and back-up guitar. Grandma and Grandpa's only child with musical talent, he could play anything he heard, almost without missing a note. He was always nice to Alissa, too, and let her play his instruments when she sat on his lap.

It was probably Alissa's interest in the music and her innate talent that endeared her to her grandparents. All the other grandkids had no interest in making music or, as Grandpa often said, "Couldn't carry a tune in a bucket." Alissa's natural abilities and insatiable curiosity put her in the thick of all that happened musically.

As the bus rumbled toward her grandparents' house, Alissa felt good about the future. She didn't think about the other things that happened at that house. Rites of passage and dark celebrations happened out at the garage at her grandparents' house, but only when they were away.

Deep within her, Alissa knew that there were other ways to live, that there was a better way for things to happen. She knew that the pain and anger that was her everyday experience didn't have to be the only way. She knew from deep inside her, the part of her she hid from the world where it was safe and happy. Her inside Sacred Place

gave her the hope she needed to believe that someday she would find that different way. Alissa knew that someday, when she had children of her own, they would never have to know the dark and evil world that she walked in every day. She KNEW all of this, but she didn't understand entirely how. It had a lot to do with White Wolf and the fuzzy memories she had of Mama and the others.

Every day it got harder to remember Mama and her sister and brothers. Every day Alissa spent more and more time inside her Sacred Place, trying to understand how things could be in so drastic a conflict. There were no answers for a young child. Alissa just KNEW there was another way. If she looked hard enough and long enough she would find it. Maybe Grandma and Grandpa could help her do just that.

Her thoughts had made her sleepy and before she knew it, Mommy was gently shaking her awake.

"Time to get off the bus, honey. Take my hand. Watch your step."

It was a short walk from the bus stop to Grandma's house. The house was dark as they approached. There was a car in the drive and a dark figure was leaning against it.

"How far did you think you'd get? Like I didn't know where you'd go!" It was Daddy's voice and Alissa shook inside, her dreams of a different way slipping out of reach.

Suddenly the door flew open and Grandma, robe flapping and barely wrapped around her nightgown, came running down the steps.

"Charles William Campbell you get right back in that there car and drive yersef home. Lori and Alissa are stayin' here tonight and y'all can work out yer differences in the morning."

That said, she put her arms around Alissa's shoulders looked Lori dead in the eye and said, "Let's go, girls. I'll make up the couch and loveseat for ya." Looking down at Alissa she said, "I'll make you some warm milk and tuck you in tight. It'll all be just fine, donchu worry 'bout nothin'!"

And they were in the house. Alissa heard her father's car rev and leave. For tonight, the world was a good place. She had convinced Grandma that it needed to be warm *chocolate* milk and the warm mug felt good in her hands.

Grandma and Mommy were in the other room, making up beds and talking low. Alissa felt sleep creep in as she imagined how it might be if this was her new world. She put her cup on the table and laid her head down. Dreams of White Wolf and Alissa the wolf cub running and playing with three other cubs filled her head. She smiled in her sleep.

Morning came early as Alissa was awakened, now on the loveseat. Someone had moved her from the kitchen and tucked her bear in close under the covers with her. Alissa smiled. She knew it was Grandma.

It was Grandma, too, who now shook her awake. "Come on, child. Gonna be late fer yer first day o' school. Can't have that, now can we? Bacon and eggs is cookin'. You get yer little butt up to the bathroom, get dressed. There's a toothbrush on the vanity waitin' fer ya. Hurry up!"

With a grin, Alissa bounced up and hurried to get ready. In the excitement of the night, she had almost forgotten today was the first day of school. In the bathroom, her new school clothes were laid out, waiting. She pulled them on with pride. These were the first brand new clothes she had ever had. All of her other things were from the Salvation Army or her cousins. These were special. The red plaid dress had a shiny belt and she even had new black and white shoes.

Dressed, teeth brushed, hair combed and grinning from ear to ear, Alissa walked into the kitchen to be greeted by her doting grandmother. Grandma fussed and primped her a little before sitting her down in front of a warm plate of bacon and eggs with toast and jelly. She tucked a napkin under Alissa's chin, with a smile, "Don't wanna get no eggs on that perty dress now do we?"

At home breakfast, if it happened at all, was a bowl of cereal with or without milk depending on what was in the fridge. Alissa got it herself and sometimes even took some to her mother. Today Mommy was still asleep on the couch, so Alissa asked, "Can I take breakfast to Mommy?"

"No, dear, we'll let her sleep. I'll take care of her later. You better hurry now. Grandpa gonna run you to school on his way to work. I'll call and get the bus to bring you up here this afternoon."

"Grandma, will I like school?"

"Oh, honey! I think you gonna be so excited. Yer already so smart, can't imagine you doin' anythin' but great! You'll be home in time to have lunch with your mom and me. It'll be just fine!"

Alissa grinned as she downed the last of her breakfast. Grandma handed her a small cloth bag with handles as she stood up. Alissa recognized the stitching. The bag had her name on it and a little red schoolhouse. Grandma must have made it especially for her. It made Alissa smile inside and out.

"Take this put any papers or things from the teacher inside it and bring it on home." She kissed the top of Alissa's head. "Go on now. Yer grampa's waitin'."

Alissa headed out the door and down the steps. Grandpa's truck was waiting for her at the end of the driveway. As she climbed in, she was sure it was going to be a great day!

Alissa was heading to Grandma's after her first day of school. It had gone well. She thought she might like her teacher, Mrs. Hancock, and her classmates were great fun. Alissa had been asked to recite the alphabet, count as high as she could, and look at words on cards. She knew she did great on her alphabet and she could count to a hundred without any help, but the words on the cards, well, she couldn't do anything with those except to tell the teacher what some of the letters she saw were. She hadn't gotten whipped or smacked, so she must not have done too poorly. She grinned. Grandma would be proud.

She scrambled off the bus and to the door as fast as she could manage, being careful to keep the papers in her bag. She walked through the front door and into the kitchen where Grandma and her mom sat at the table. Aunt Jean and Aunt Susie were there, too. Alissa stopped herself at the doorway, waiting to be acknowledged since children were to be seen and not heard.

"Don't stand there in the door, child! Come in and tell Gramma all about yer first day!"

Alissa bounded into her grandmother's open arms and began telling her all about the fun things she had done and how she hadn't

gotten into any trouble all day! Grandma smiled and said, "That's great, dear. Why don't you take these warm cookies and this glass o' milk outside. I'll bring yer san'wich out fer ya in a minute. Your cousins will be here as soon as their school day is over. Go on now. Go outside and play."

Happily, Alissa grabbed three warm oatmeal cookies off the counter near the stove and the cup of milk waiting for her. She headed out the back door. The women at the table waited for the bang of the door to confirm the child had indeed left the room.

"You know that's one hell of a kid ya got there, Lori." It was Jean who had three kids of her own, two girls and a boy.

"Yeah, she just always seems to be underfoot and getting' into stuff she shouldn't. She knows the rules and breaks them anyway."

"Well, her daddy weren't no angel neither. Whudaya expect?" Lori's mother-in-law, Roz, had always treated her well. She had no illusions about the son she had raised and the trouble he could be. Last night had been a true test and Roz had come through, protecting Lori and Alissa from her own flesh and blood. Lori knew that had not been easy. She smiled now as the table rumbled with talk between the two sisters and their mother about the trouble the six kids had been for their mother over the years.

"So, whadaya gonna do now?" It was Susie's turn to query. She looked at Lori and waited for a response.

"Well, I can go back to my folks' house, I guess. Got some fences to mend with my stepfather, but I think it'll be okay."

"What about Chuck? Ain't like he gonna just give up on you and that young 'un. He needs her. And you!"

"Needs us?"

"Yeah, you know what I mean."

Lori did. The Organization had strict rules about allowing its members to leave. It wasn't permitted. As the local leader, Chuck had a reputation to protect. He was going to have to keep Lori and Alissa on a short leash. Lori thought she could work it out with him, pledging her services and that of Alissa. She knew it was going to take some work, but she thought she could work it out. IF she could keep him sober long enough to discuss it and make him understand. She had already sold her soul to the Devil; why not sell her life to his henchman?

Chapter 9: New Life, Old Rules...

Living with Gram and Papaw was proving to be a little more difficult than Alissa had hoped. It was very different than Grandma's house. This was Mommy's mom and stepfather. This was *their* house. They made that quite clear. Also, Alissa had thought that things would be different, better here than before. It did not seem to be going as well as she had hoped.

Sure, school was great. Kindergarten was proving to be easy for her and she almost never got into trouble. Sometimes Mrs. Hancock would yell at her for talking too much, but there was no sign of a belt and no one looking to stick things inside her. That was all very good. There were the days she could walk to and from home, leaving after breakfast and getting home in time for lunch. Then there were the days when Daddy picked her up.

Mom had set it up that Dad picked Alissa up Mondays, Wednesdays, and Fridays. She was with him over the weekend so was really only with Gram and Papaw Tuesdays and Thursdays. The rest of the time she was with her father. He always had friends at the house and Alissa was always expected to "take care" of those friends.

No one at home or school asked much about the bruises. Alissa knew the answers if anyone did, "I tripped down the stairs." "I fell out of the tree." Plenty of pat answers, sometimes specific stories given to her so she knew exactly what to say. Mostly, no one asked.

It was Tuesday and she was home from school and with Gram.

Gram's afternoon shows were on, so Alissa was expected to keep quiet and could only speak when the commercials came on. She waited patiently for the next commercial to ask if she could go outside and play with Danny, the boy who lived behind the house. He was 4 and didn't go to school just yet. They had great fun.

The next commercial Alissa ventured, "Can I go out and play with Danny, Gram?"

"Stay off the grass. You know Papaw will tan your hide if you step on his lawn."

"Okay. Bye."

Out the door to the driveway, Alissa was careful to stay on the sidewalk until she was to the corner. Turning that corner, she raced up the block to Danny's house, hoping he was home. Danny had a younger brother, David, and two older sisters who were never around. Danny and Alissa had become great friends. They played tag and army together. The houses down Danny's street were just far enough apart they could jump from garage to garage all the way down the block. It was dangerous but fun. There were no scary rules here and sometimes Alissa even got to eat lunch at Danny's house. That was great. His house was a lot more like Grandma's house. It smelled good and was warm and cozy with hugs and cookies.

All these thoughts raced through Alissa's head as she dashed to play with her friend. At least today, life was good.

It was Friday and the kindergarten half-day was over. The kids were all heading outside to wait for their rides home. Alissa knew Daddy was coming to get her. She knew this was a Full moon weekend and she KNEW she didn't want to go. As she came down the steps, she spotted Eric. She and Eric did not get along too well and she knew it wouldn't take much to get him to engage with her. As she rushed past him, she pushed him, hard, down the steps. As he picked himself up, obviously angry, he turned on her. They were locked in a fistfight in a matter of seconds.

It took the adults in the area about three minutes to realize what was happening and another five to actually get the two children

apart. They were marched immediately to the office where they sat in the chairs outside the principal's office. Eric glowered at Alissa. She could almost feel the heat of his anger as he stared at her, arms crossed tightly across his chest. She wanted to tell him she was sorry, that it didn't have anything to do with him, but she knew that was useless. She just glared back, aware that her survival in this inner city school would depend on her ability to appear able to take care of herself.

She had been jumped for the first time within the first few weeks of school. The three older kids who jumped her were looking to establish fear so they could intimidate her and take what they wanted, usually money. As a kindergartner, she didn't have lunch money, but they were laying the groundwork now so they didn't have to deal with her later. Fortunately for Alissa, they were nothing compared to the monsters in her home life. She had fought back. Although she had sustained a black eye, bruised ribs and a skinned shin, they had walked away with a little more respect for her. Soon after that she started carrying an old pocketknife she had found in one of Papaw's toolboxes in the garage. The next time they came at her, she pulled it out, having opened it in anticipation. They had backed down and had not bothered her since. She still kept the little knife close by. She had practiced with it and was pretty good. She taught Danny how to use it and soon they began playing games to improve their skill. She touched it in the pocket of her jeans as she sat in the principal's chair, waiting for Eric to come out. It wouldn't help her here, but touching it gave her the strength she needed when facing the ominous man behind the door.

The door opened and Eric came out, eyes wet with tears. Obviously there had been a paddling administered. Alissa had not yet been paddled, though she had heard the threats. She wasn't sure what it meant, but had the familiar fear in the pit of her stomach. It was the same fear that overtook her when she knew she would be whipped when Mommy got home. She swallowed hard as she entered the principal's office.

"So, young lady, what seems to be the problem? I understand from Eric and some of the other teachers that you were the instigator today. Want to tell me about it?"

"My daddy is coming to pick me up and I don't want to go with him."

"So you started a fight to not have to leave the school?"

"I guess."

"Well, that doesn't make much sense. Why wouldn't you want to go with your father?"

"Because he fucks me and it hurts and I don't wanna do that any more."

"Now listen here. Telling those kind of lies you'll go to hell. That kind of language is unacceptable here. You have two swats coming for fighting and I'm gonna add three more for the language and lying. Now stand up and bend over, grab your ankles and I'll give you your five swats and then we'll call home."

Alissa bit back the tears, not because of the swats. The principal had a wooden board that he used on her bottom, fully clothed, five times. It was nothing compared to the beatings at home, she barely even felt it. But he had said he was calling home. That would mean a significant beating at home and at Daddy's house. She shuddered at the thought.

The principal assumed Alissa's contrite behavior was due to his reprimand. He never really heard her words, or he wouldn't allow himself to hear it. Such things didn't really happen. It was all the over active imagination of a young child. He dialed the phone. Alissa shook by his side.

"So, got yourself in trouble at school, eh? Fightin'. I told ya, you get yourself in trouble at school and it'll be worse here. Ya got five swats from the principal, that right?"

"Yes, sir."

"So whadda ya thinkin' I should do with ya?"

Alissa didn't answer. He backhanded her in the mouth.

"I'm talkin' to ya, bitch, answer me!"

"I don't know, sir."

"Sure ya do. Go in that back room and get my belt. Come out here, pull your pants to your ankles and bend over."

Alissa moved to the back room, head down. He kept the belt he used to whip her in the back closet. It was an old leather belt with holes the full length for more sting. Sometimes, when she was really bad, he would wet it before he used it. Alissa knew that this was better than the beating she could've gotten had he been drunk when he picked her up. She grabbed the belt and headed back to him.

"Drop your pants. And what do you tell me?"

"I'm sorry, Daddy, for being bad. Please whip me so I won't be bad anymore."

He began his retribution to her bare bottom. Alissa didn't know when he would stop. She felt his excitement rise as the blows got harder. The belt landed on her legs and back. His breathing began to change. When he finally stopped, he turned her around. His pants were down and he was hard.

"Now suck it good so it can go into your ass. Don't go in so good until its nice and hard."

Alissa closed her eyes as he entered her mouth. She gave gratitude for her Sacred Place.

When Alissa turned 7 it was decided that she was old enough to take on more responsibility around the house. She now was expected to help wash, dry and put away the dishes after dinner and clean Papaw's upstairs bathroom once a week. This was in addition to cleaning the downstairs bathroom, cleaning the room she and Mommy shared and taking out the trash.

Overall, Alissa didn't mind the chores. She was used to the ones she had done since they arrived. They weren't hard. Doing dishes was kind of fun. Mommy helped sometimes and they could talk. Other times Alissa did them alone. With a step stool, she could reach the sink and any dishes she couldn't reach to put away she left on the table and Gram took care of them.

But cleaning Papaw's bathroom was scary. Papaw had his own bedroom and living area, with full bathroom, upstairs. Gram had her room downstairs and Mommy and Alissa shared the other bedroom downstairs. Unless Alissa had a really bad day, then she might end up

in the basement in the dark room for the night. Those were the nights Alissa chose to go inside and sleep in her Sacred Place instead of being outside with the dark and dank space. Sometimes Spider would visit and Alissa would talk with her. She told her stories and Alissa listened, pleased for the company.

Cleaning Papaw's bathroom was her Thursday chore. After school, before she could go out and play, Alissa would gather the cleaning supplies and head upstairs. If Papaw was not there, all was well and she would hurry to finish before he might arrive. She had to be careful since, if her chores were not done well enough, Mommy would take the strap to her bare hide.

If Papaw was up there, it meant she would have to touch him and play with him, sucking him till he came. He was never hurtful like Daddy and his friends, but it was not pleasant and Alissa hated how it made her feel. She knew it was not how it was supposed to be... at least she thought she knew it. It was getting harder and harder to remember that there was another way. Didn't all of her classmates and friends have the same experience? Don't all daddies teach their daughters like Allisa's did? She knew Danny's dad took a belt to him sometimes, too. So, maybe this really was how it was supposed to be. Maybe.

Chapter 10: Sacred Place

Alissa had successfully created her own safe place, a place she could go when life outside was unbearable. By closing her eyes, she could go to her Sacred Place where there were others to play with and talk with. White Wolf, Bear and Eagle lived here. Spider came here to visit her. Sometimes Alissa would stay in her Sacred Place for so long she would forget about the world outside, the hurting and scary things that happened all the time. Sometimes she would find herself in the outside world in places she didn't know. She found she didn't remember how she got there and even who the people were around her. This could sometimes be dangerous, since knowing the rules and expectations was always critical for survival. But even those difficulties were not enough to prevent Alissa from closing her eyes and going deep inside to her Sacred Place.

Nothing bad ever happened here. There were no rules, no one to force her to do things she didn't want to do. There was only softness, good feelings and loving arms here. Who could blame Alissa for wanting to be here when outside was such a risky place? More and more time went by when Alissa would almost forget to go back outside the safety she had found. Over time, it got harder and harder to leave. Alissa never thought about what that meant to the outside world. All she knew was how it felt here.

She knew that within that inside world, just past the mountains there was a darker place, a place where others lived, those put there

by someone else. But she didn't think about that too much. She stayed away from the edges of that place, here where it was safe and warm.

Waterfalls, mountains, green grass, sunshine… it was all there. And it was hers for the enjoyment. She had hollow trees that she and the others played, napped and dreamed within. There was a nursery room that rocked and had all the soft toys you could dream up. There was a babbling creek with frogs and crayfish, minnows and cattails. Sunsets and sunrises were always beautiful. Even when it rained, it was a place that never felt scary or dangerous. Alissa loved it here. Maybe a little too much.

"Do you find Alissa difficult to deal with at home sometimes?"

It was Alissa's first grade teacher talking on the phone to Gram.

"No. We keep her pretty well under our thumb when she's here. Her father has her a lot, though. Sometimes after she's been there, she can be a handful. Why? What kind of trouble is she getting into there?"

"It isn't that she's getting into trouble, really. She's a bit mischievous and ornery and can be a handful at times, but that's not what I'm talking about. I see significant moodiness some days. She behaves in ways that are… unusual. Like she's not always herself. I know that sounds funny. I just wondered if you saw anything at home."

"I'm not sure what you're talking about. We don't see any of that here. Maybe she's just tired. She was sick about two weeks ago. Maybe she just hasn't fully recovered."

"Well, maybe that's it. I just wanted to touch base with you and see what you thought."

"I think you worry too much. Why don't you just stick to reading and writing? Alissa having any trouble with her studies?"

"No, none at all. She's an A student."

"Good. Then you're doing a great job. Thanks for calling. Bye."

Chapter 11: Taking Care of Yourself...

It was Sunday night, the Sunday night after the full moon, the Sunday night after her rite of passage. At the age of 7, Alissa had now endured three rites of passage. Rites of passage were about abuse and endurance, training and programming. It was during the rites of passage that the messages were solidified. It was here that young bodies, taken to within inches of life through torture and rape, were told they were worthless, only served as victims, destined for this life alone and locked within this life because if they chose to leave they would die. Some didn't make it through their rites. That was part of the purpose. The Organization had learned how to weed through and mold and design their victims, manipulating and brainwashing by taking these young members to their limits, and the younger the better. They had found that by the time victims were 5 years old it was too late. If they had not grown up in this world, exposed to things gradually before the age of 5, they died quickly. It's not like they TRIED to kill them, they just didn't notice if they did.

The purpose of the rites was to ensure that victims moved through the process to become members in good standing; perpetrators. The Organization supported itself through the sale of drugs, guns, slaves, prostitutes, stolen property and child pornography. Members in good standing were willing to take part in one or more of these venues and enjoy their work. Such involvement guaranteed loyalty because of the promise of great rewards such as sex, drugs and money or the

threat of self-incrimination, blame and punishment. The only way to achieve such members was to start young or happen upon those who could be bought later with drugs, sex and money. This made The Organization a self-perpetuating industry, never lacking for those willing to be a part at some level. Not that all members were welcome within the full strata of The Organization. There were those who served only within the monetary structures, never interested in venturing further. Others enjoyed some power as a boss, thus moving within the infrastructure. Those at the top knew that there was much to be said about the advantages of working for the Devil.

An integral part of The Organization, Alissa was too young to understand all this. She did know that rites of passage were to be endured if one was to survive. She was willing to do anything to continue to survive, no matter how awful life was. It was true there were moments she prayed to die, but those prayers were never answered and most days she was adamant she would survive to spite these bad guys. In the movies, the good guys always won. Somehow, she knew she was one of the good guys and HAD to survive.

This particular Sunday, her survival was threatened. Despite Marge's attempts to pack off the vaginal and anal bleeding, Alissa's underwear was stained when she got home. As the high from the narcotics wore off, she began to feel the pain inside her. She knew something was not right.

It was late. She could hear Mommy in the bed nearby. Her breathing indicating she was asleep. Alissa crept to the door. She looked out at Gram's door. It was closed and no light came from under it. Papaw's upstairs lights were also off. Everyone appeared asleep.

Walking gently to cause herself the least amount of pain, Alissa tiptoed through the house. She went through the change jar by the front door and got out what she needed for the bus. She had been to the free clinic several times before, always with a different adult. She was pretty sure she knew how to get there by herself. It was the only way to guarantee her survival and not cost her more pain. She closed the door gently behind her as she left the house.

The night air felt good and gave her a little more strength. She wasn't sure when the next bus would come, but she hurried to the stop so as not to miss it. It seemed a long time before it finally arrived. As she boarded the bus, the driver gave her a bit of a stare, but said nothing. Alissa found a seat and sank down, glad for slight relief from the pain. She knew she had to connect to the next bus to get to the clinic. She hoped she could get there and back before it was time for school.

The registering nurse at the clinic had Alissa sit on the cold chair next to her desk as she ducked behind the rickety door. When she came back, she was not alone. Alissa recognized the man with her.

"Well, look who we have here. Why don't you come on back with me? We'll get you all fixed up."

Alissa took his hand as they went to the back. She laid on the hard table, barely covered by a sheet.

Noticing the blood now staining her jeans, the man said, "Had a rough weekend, huh?"

Alissa nodded.

"We'll get you fixed up. Lay back. Take this. It'll make you sleepy and when you wake up, everything will be better. That's a good girl."

Alissa took the pill and water from the man. She watched as he used a tourniquet on her arm and gave her a shot into her vein. She felt the world go fuzzy, then felt nothing at all.

When she woke up, she was covered with a sheet and thin blanket. She was naked beneath the bedclothes and unsure of where she was. As she oriented herself, the man came back in.

"Ah, you're awake. It was good of you to come down. We patched you up, but you need to rest a little longer."

That said, he inserted another needle in her arm. Alissa slipped away. It was okay. She liked the feeling. Not as good as her Sacred Place, but being high was always better than facing life for real. It was a familiar friend, given to her for as long as she could remember. If she had to be here, high was how she liked it. She let it take over.

The next thing she knew she was being shaken awake.

"Okay, sleepy. Let's get you dressed. Take this bag for later. You can use it when the stuff we gave you wears off. Gonna get yourself home now, okay?"

Groggy but aware, Alissa nodded. She felt better with the drugs in her. She knew she could do almost anything. Fully dressed with her stash in her pocket, she left the clinic and waited for the bus. Orienting herself outside, she saw a newspaper the man next to her at the bus stop had and realized it was Tuesday. Looking for the time, she realized she would need to go directly to school. She wondered who had missed her yesterday and what the impacts would be. Those thoughts haunted her as she boarded the bus.

"Okay. This stuff goes to 151 Main Street. Can you remember that?"

"Dad, I been runnin' stuff for you for the last two years. I think I can handle the address."

At 8 years old, Alissa was well versed in the art of drug trade. She served as the mule, less likely to be stopped or suspected by the cops. Her job was to take the stuff from the supplier to the buyer. There she was often expected to use just enough of it to prove it was good shit. "Stuff" could be any of about ten or twelve illegal substances and Alissa knew well how to use them all.

"Okay, Speed, just remember the second drop is in the alley by the Waffle Wagon."

Her father had taken to calling her Speed since she could move the stuff at a pretty good clip. Truth be told, Alissa liked the stuff she delivered and knew the faster she moved it the more she got to deliver which meant the more she got to use. Seemed like a win-win to her!

"Got it, Dad. After that where do I go?"

"Head over to Uncle John's. He has a job for you."

She was not pleased to hear that. However, with any luck, after the first two stops she would be high enough to put up with Uncle John's bullshit. Whatever it was. She headed out the door, school bag over her shoulder.

Alissa thought about how the drugs helped her get through the day to day. It was as if she floated through. There were times, like when she had to do the pictures, drugs were used as incentive. It was her reward for doing exactly what the photographer wanted. Sometimes it was her reward for doing the photographer. Whatever it took, Alissa was generally quite willing to do it to get high. High was much better than facing reality sober.

There were other times, when she just had to have a fix, that she would sneak it from her father's stash. She knew how dangerous that was. If her father ever found out it could be fatal. As the Dargon, her father had a reputation to keep and superiors to which he answered. Messing with his stuff put his life in jeopardy. So she was always careful not to take too much, and not from the same place. Generally speaking, drugs were available other ways, so she didn't have to do it often. But she had to take care of herself, after all, no one else would.

Chapter 12: Unheeded Cries...

"Mrs. Campbell?"

"Yes?"

"This is Mr. Whitehall, the Principal. We think Alissa may have ingested something toxic. The ambulance is on the way. We'll need you to meet them at the Emergency Room as soon as possible."

"I'll finish here at work and be on my way."

"Mrs. Campbell, she's unconscious. We don't know what she's ingested. We suspect she's tried to kill herself."

"She's only 8. How could that be possible? I'll get there as quickly as possible. Thank you."

Lori paused. What was that child thinking?

Alissa knew the dangers of taking too much heroin. But it seemed too hard to go on. She had seen and been a part of awful things this weekend. She felt awful. She wasn't sure she wanted to go on living. Who would miss her? Her father could replace her with any whore. Her mother barely noticed her. People at school thought she was simply a pain in their ass. She couldn't think of any real reason to be alive. The good thing about heroin, which was not the DTs it caused, was that a little too much and she would just cease to exist. How hard could it be?

So, she set herself up behind the school. It was quiet there with the bushes just high enough that no one would see her until it was too

late. She hit her arm with it, slid the stuff under the bush. As she felt the high take over, she just laid down.

She was on her own island, floating, just being. She heard voices around her, but they didn't appeal to her. She ignored them, happy in the high. The island awoke and welcomed her, opened its arms to her. She stepped in. Then everything went wrong. The island, moments ago serene and welcoming, became a black hole sucking her in, threatening with large teeth to chew her up. Fearing the pain, she screamed and turned to run. The teeth dug into her and she felt the pain throughout her flesh. In the grasp of this dark, unknown monster she wrenched and screamed, begging for it to let her go, begging to die. The fight went on. She screamed. It roared. She cried. It chewed on her. When darkness finally came, Alissa could not even feel comfortable in the nothingness.

"We almost lost you, kiddo."

It was her mother. At least that's what she thought. Her head hurt and her eyes couldn't focus. All she saw was a bright, white light and fuzzy faces. She tried to speak, but nothing came out.

"It's okay. Sleep for now. We'll get you settled and talk about it later."

This was not a voice she knew. But for now, she didn't have the energy to care. Her head heavy, body aching, she fell into a fitful sleep filled with more horrors and dreams, these of the familiar abuse and perpetrators with names.

"We have to put her on 24 hour suicide observation, ma'am. I'm sorry. It's protocol."

"She's 8-years-old. She came across some interesting stuff and decided to try it. How hard is that for you to understand? I'm her mother, for god's sake. I'll take her home and keep an eye on her myself."

"She has a broken arm and several broken ribs and bruises all over the place. We think it would be better if we kept her, just until tomorrow."

"We live in a rough neighborhood. She's had trouble before. I'm sure she can tell us all about it when she feels better. She will feel better faster at home. I demand that you release her!"

"I can't do that ma'am. I'm sorry."

"Get me the hospital administrator. I want to talk to the man in charge!"

"Yes, ma'am."

Lori was frustrated and angry. Alissa had pulled this stunt for attention, no doubt and all these people wanted to do was probe into their private business. Lori knew the hospital administrator would see it her way.

"Well, hello, Lori. Problem?"

"Hi Roy. Good to see you. Alissa pulled a stunt and wound up here at your hospital. The guys downstairs won't let me take her home. I was hoping you could talk reason into them."

"No problem. I'll talk to them immediately. You'll be sure to let Chuck know how helpful I've been, won't you?"

"Of course, I will."

Lori knew Roy was hoping for a promotion within The Organization. The more leverage she could muster, the better.

"Thanks so much for your help, Roy."

"No thanks necessary. Take that child home and take care of her."

"You know I will. Chuck will want to make sure he has a chance to take care of her, too."

"I'm sure. Let me take care of this little matter. By the time you get back downstairs, all should be taken care of."

"Great. I'll give your best to Chuck."

Lori smiled as she entered the elevator. Knowing the players was definitely a blessing. There were a lot of people in positions of power throughout the city and her relationship with Chuck, tenuous as it was, made her privy to who and where. Though she tried not to abuse it, Chuck would agree how important this move had been. Had Alissa gone upstairs to the psychiatric unit, the wrong person may have asked the wrong questions and it could bring unnecessary pressure to

The Organization. That was not good for any of them. Lori had done them all a favor. She would be sure to let Chuck know about Roy's cooperation. It would work out well for everyone.

As she exited the elevator, she saw Alissa, half awake in a wheelchair with a nurse, waiting for her.

"She's all ready to go, Mrs. Campbell. Remember to keep that arm elevated and she needs an appointment with the orthopedic within the next two days to get that arm set before it starts to heal. All the information for contacting him is on the discharge report. Sign right here."

"Thank you. We'll take care of that first thing in the morning. Have a great day!"

"Thanks, you too."

And they were out of there. Alissa sat in her gloom and pain. She had hoped for escape and had only managed to make things worse. She knew the repercussions would be severe. With a cast on her right arm almost to her armpit, she wasn't in much shape to defend herself. She sighed deeply, closed her eyes and found her Sacred Place.

It was late. The basement was well lit with photographers' lights. Mattresses were strewn here and there. Children of all ages lined the walls, laid on the mattresses or stood where they were told, all of them naked, most of them tear-stained. Some had bruises or red marks, evidence of failed duties. Alissa, at 8 years old, was considered one of the older children. She was expected to perpetrate a younger child as often as she was expected to accept being perpetrated. She was not very good at it. Her heart hurt to see the younger children's pain and fear. On more than one occasion she had refused to hurt another child. The retribution meant a severe beating from two or three of the men. They also often forced objects into several of her orifices, sometimes causing them to bleed. Then, arm twisted to breaking point behind her back, she was led to the Box.

The Box was a small cabinet, only big enough to allow Alissa to sit or kneel. There was not enough room to turn around or stand up. The floor was strewn with marbles that had been cemented into the tiles

of the floor. This meant it quickly became painful, no matter how you positioned yourself. After the beatings, little was required to make the pain unbearable. Once there, someone had to remember where you were to come and ask if you were ready to cooperate. The most Alissa had ever been able to tolerate was two rounds of the Box before she had to comply with her captors.

Today, she had withstood one round in the Box before she felt at her limits. Once released, she stood against the wall, awaiting directions. There was a loud crash.

"Police!

"Freeze!"

"Don't move!"

Screams and running feet surrounded her. Alissa was unsure what to do. All her life she had heard that if they were ever caught it would be all her fault and she would be the one to get into trouble. But her feet wouldn't obey her commands to run. Her body hurt too much to argue. She crumpled to a ball on the floor, leaning against the wall, rocking in fear, hands over her head in protection.

"I've got another one over here! Hey, honey, I won't hurt you. See, I'm a cop."

Alissa had no reason to believe that a cop meant safety. She lived in the inner city. She ran drugs as the family business. She knew several of the cops, including some higher-ups, that were on the take. She had no reason to believe the man before her. She didn't move.

Feeling a blanket around her shoulders, head buried in her arms, she heard him say, "It's okay. We'll get you out of here and someplace safe."

Before she knew it she was being lifted. She looked around and could see no one familiar. She saw kids, but where were the adults? Each child was wrapped in a blanket and had a cop nearby. What was going on?

The officer carried her outside and placed her in the backseat of a cruiser. As she sat there, she thought she saw a flash of light from the bushes, like a lighter or a flashlight. But she wasn't sure. She saw other policemen leading many of the men who had served as perpetrators

in handcuffs to a big police wagon. Most of them were barely covered and the cops didn't seem interested in providing them with much more. The cameras and lights were being carried to another vehicle she couldn't see. Lots of official looking people milled in and out of the building. Alissa knew there had to have been a leak from within The Organization for the cops to show up like this. She also knew that the leak had to be linked to the cops somehow; otherwise those cops who belonged to The Organization would have been able to prevent this from happening.

There would be a search within The Organization to find the rat responsible for this raid. Alissa had seen searches for rats before. It was not pleasant. Lots of people died, some innocently. Ultimately, someone was blamed. Punishment was delivered publicly at a one of the big Conventions. That was how they made sure there were examples. Everyone needed to know what happened if you sold out or tried to get out. There was no life except for that within The Organization. Once there, you stayed there.

Alissa was shaken back to reality by a gentle voice.

"Hello there."

The woman was blonde, hair a bit askew as if she had been roused from bed. She probably was. After all, it must be pretty late.

"Can you tell me your name?"

"Why?"

"So I know what to call you."

"My father calls me Speed."

"Its nice to meet you Speed. Who is your father?"

"Dargon."

"I see. Would it be okay if I took you to the hospital to get checked over and make sure you are okay?"

"No. I'm fine. Please don't take me to the hospital. I just want to go home and go to bed."

"Where's home?"

Speed couldn't remember anything right now. "I don't know."

"Okay. Well, let's get you someplace safe and warm for tonight. We can deal with everything else in the morning. Okay?"

Speed liked the woman. She had a nice smile. "Okay."

The woman took Speed's hand and they walked over to another car, this one light blue with a white roof. Speed sat in the front seat. They drove for a while before the woman stopped. She took Speed's hand and they walked to the front door of a large house. A burly man opened the door.

"Hello, Elaine." His voice was not what Speed expected with the gruff appearance. He spoke softly and gently.

"Hi, Bill. This is Speed. That's all she seems to know right now. Thought she might be able to stay with you tonight. I'll get paperwork started in the morning and sift through the details of whatever the police have to say and where we think she belongs. That okay with you?"

"Sure. Have an extra bed upstairs." He yelled over his shoulder, "Greta, make up the upstairs bed. We have a young guest tonight."

There was movement inside the house as they walked through the door.

"Don't worry. We'll take care of her tonight. Call and let us know in the morning what to do next. Now you need to go on home and go to bed, as well."

"Thanks, Bill. I'll call as soon as I know anything."

The door closed behind them.

"Let's get you settled in for the night. Don't look like you have much with you."

Speed looked down and realized she only had the blanket the policeman had given her covering her. She pulled it a little tighter around her, unsure if this man meant her harm.

"It's all right. I have a shirt you can sleep in. Greta will help you figure out what to do in the morning. You got a bit of a bruise there on your cheek. Need anything for that?"

"No, sir. May I take a shower before I go to bed?"

"My, my. You have some nice manners there. I think we can get you a towel and a shower before bed. Greta? Can you get a clean towel for Speed?"

"I'm putting sheets on the bed. Can you get the towel, please?"

"Sure," he hollered to Greta. "Wait here," he directed Speed.

They had stopped on the landing of the upstairs hallway. Bill had opened the door to the left, a linen closet, and pulled out a fluffy yellow towel. Handing it to Speed he said, "This should do. Here's a washcloth. Bathroom is right there to your right. I'll go get that shirt and have it on the vanity for you when you finish. Okay?"

It had been a long time since anyone had been this nice to Speed. She smiled, nodded and went into the bathroom. She began running warm water. There was a gentle knock. Bill reached only his arm into the bathroom.

"Here's that shirt. Wish I had more to offer you. We'll show you to your room when you're done."

Speed took the shirt and placed it on the vanity. Bill closed the door. As she let the blanket fall to the floor she saw herself in the full-length mirror behind the door. She had cuts, bumps and bruises all over her face and body. No wonder people had seemed worried. In her real life, she always wore clothes to cover the body bruises. The fights and scuffles at school and in the neighborhood could explain the other marks. Not that anyone asked. Not where she lived or who her father was. As she lowered herself into the warm water, she sensed this place was different.

Three days with Bill and Greta Miller and Speed felt like a brand new person. Because she continued to call herself only by the name 'Speed' it was taking time for the authorities to piece things together. She had a new pair of jeans, two new sweatshirts, socks, underwear and a new pair of tennis shoes. She felt like a princess.

To Speed's amazement, they sat at the dinner table each night with their son, Chris, and Speed. They talked and laughed and seemed to truly enjoy each other. Speed had thought about that and the gentle loving things that happened every day in this house. There was a risk, but she thought it was worth taking. So, just before dinner that night, she touched Bill on the shoulder, "Can I talk to you for a minute?"

"Sure, Speed. What do you need?"

"I don't want to go home."

"Well, that's been pretty obvious since you won't tell us what your real name is."

"That's the only name I can remember." She wasn't lying.

"Okay. It's all gonna be fine. Don't worry. Was that what you wanted to tell me?"

"No. I wanted to tell you that my father, he does mean things to me. I don't like it and I want it to stop. Can you help me?"

"Maybe. I'm gonna have Greta come in here, too. Okay?"

"Uh huh."

Greta came in, concern on her face.

"Bill told me what you said. We can help you if you're willing to talk to someone. You can talk to us, but you have to talk to someone else who can really help you. Remember Elaine? The woman who brought you here?"

"Yes."

"If we stay with you, will you talk to her?"

"I think so. I don't want anyone to whip me, please!"

Greta looked shocked, "Oh, no, child! That won't happen here. I can promise you that. And Elaine will do no such thing, either. Bill, you want give her a call. See if she can come over this evening. The sooner the better."

"Okay, dear. Can we eat dinner first? Don't want it to get cold."

"You go call from the den. I'll get dinner on the table. That way it all gets done at the same time."

"Always the organized one, eh?" Bill smiled as he went to the den.

"Come on. Let's get dinner before it gets cold."

Tentatively, Speed followed Greta. It was hard to believe there were no whippings or beatings for what she had said. She had been afraid of the risks, but she just had to try. White Wolf had reminded her the night before that there was another way, that what the Millers showed her was part of it. The only way she might be able to reach it, to have it, was to take risks. So far, her risk had paid off.

Dinner was a little more quiet than usual. Chris talked about his day at school. He was just in kindergarten and talked about the

exciting things they did. His innocence made Speed smile. She didn't see that often.

After dinner, Greta went up to put Chris to bed early. She promised him an extra story and one more cookie if he would go to bed at 7:30 instead of 8:00. Chris eagerly agreed.

Speed was helping Bill with the dishes when the front door bell rang. Speed looked at Bill, fear creeping into her eyes.

"It'll be okay, Speed. Remember, Greta and I are here with you. I'm sure that's Elaine. Put those last plates away and let's go into the den."

He put down his dishcloth, hollered up to Greta that Elaine was here, and headed for the door. Speed felt panic grab her throat as she walked to the den.

She froze at the door. Seated on the couch were Elaine and a man who was very familiar to Speed. He was one of Dargon's right hand men. Seeing her, Elaine rose and walked to her.

"Speed, Bill and Greta told me you had something you wanted to talk about. Some things you wanted to tell us about why you don't want to go home. Policy at my agency requires two workers to take down the information. Leon here will be the other worker on this case. I hope that's okay."

Speed didn't answer. She knew if she talked about anything of the horrors at home, Leon would tell her father and she would become a scapegoat. Her thoughts raced, the rules played like a tape over and over.

"No noise. No tears. No tell."

"No tell."

"No tell."

"No tell."

She was losing control. She felt herself slipping away. The Sacred Place came into view.

Chapter 13: The Worlds Collide...

Alissa looked around the room. How had she gotten here? Who were these people? She recognized Leon and looked to him for a clue. He just stared at her, almost looking through her.

"Go on, honey. What is it you wanted to tell us?" The gentle words came from an older woman to her right. "We told you we would stay with you. It's okay. These are people who want to help you."

"Give her a minute, Greta." The big man standing behind the couch spoke softly. "I'm sure it's all a little scary for her. When you're ready, Speed. Tell us when you're ready."

Alissa raced to understand the situation. Obviously these people were waiting to hear something from her. What could that be? And what was the talk of people wanting to help? Leon was here. He was anything but helpful, except, of course, for himself. Overwhelmed, she fainted.

"Poor child. Just too much for one so young." Greta shook her head as she spoke.

As Alissa came to, she saw that the same faces surrounded her. She still had no idea what was going on, but quickly devised a plan.

"I feel very tired now. I'd like to go to bed. Can we talk tomorrow, please?"

"We got these nice people to come by tonight because it seemed to us important that you tell them why you don't want to go home.

We figured it might help them figure out where you belong and what steps to take to keep you safe." The big man spoke again.

"We know where she belongs," Leon stated. "We were able to determine who her family is. We were planning to contact them tomorrow to let them know that she's safe and make arrangements for their reunification."

"Do you hear that, Speed? Is that what you want?" It was the woman called Greta.

"I guess. If that's what's best."

"Hold on here. I'm not so sure that's the best thing. What about what you told me earlier? About your father?"

"Yes, tell us what you told Bill about your father," Leon leaned forward as he said this. Alissa could see the clear message in his eyes. The rules. Don't forget the rules.

"I... I don't know what you're talking about. Of course I want to go home. Can you call my family tonight?"

"I'm sure they'd be happy to have you come home as soon as possible. Elaine, do you think we could make that phone call right now and maybe even drop the child off tonight?"

"Umm... that's not really how procedure works, Leon. You know that."

"Yeah, but if your child had been missing wouldn't you want to see her as soon as possible?"

"I suppose. But I would rather follow protocol. Speed, do you think you could wait until morning to see your family? I'll take care of all the details, myself, in the morning. This is all a little confusing and I would like the chance to talk to Leon about how it is he knows so much more than I do." She glanced in Leon's direction.

"When you called, I was in the office. I grabbed the file off your desk and all the information is in there. It must have been waiting for you. The full police report and all the information is there. Here."

Leon handed the file to Elaine.

"So, Speed, it seems your real name is Alissa Campbell. You live with your mother and her parents. I have their contact information right here. What I don't have is an explanation as to how you ended up where you did the other night. Do you have any insight, Alissa?"

"I… I… I'm not sure."

Alissa wasn't sure where she had ended up or how. The last thing she remembered she was in the Box. After that, she had no idea what had taken place.

"Okay. I see a trauma reaction here. Leon, I think we need to slow things down. Let's talk about this in the morning. Unless Alissa has something more she wants to say, I think we should call it a night."

"Alissa?" Bill looked at the child, hopeful.

"Yes, sir?"

"Are you sure you don't have anything more you want to say to Elaine before she leaves and makes arrangements for you to go home?"

"Yes, sir. I'm sure."

She lowered her head, feeling exhausted and confused. This is what happened when she went to her Sacred Place and stayed for a long time. All Alissa wanted to do was go to bed and sort things out in her head.

"I'm very tired. May I go to bed?"

"Of course, child." It was Greta. "I'll take you and we can get ready."

As they left the room, Alissa heard Leon say to Bill, "The kid is obviously a little confused and maybe even delusional. I don't know that anything she says is credible. After all, she didn't even tell you her real name. We'll take care of things and do a full investigation before we return her to the home. In the meantime, just keep her safe and quiet. We'll get in touch with you tomorrow."

Alissa sat in a very white waiting room. This was some kind of a shrink who was supposed to assess whether or not she had been traumatized. Leon sat beside her. She hadn't seen Elaine since last night. Leon had picked her up at the house and brought her here. Alissa had figured out that she had said something to Bill and Greta about home not being a place she wanted to be and something about her father. That was based on what was said last night and the conversation Bill and Greta had around her that morning.

Silence was the rule. Alissa knew that telling the secrets meant certain death. She had seen her father and the others kill for saying less.

She was afraid of what repercussions she already stood to experience. She didn't really know how much she had said already and to whom. She looked up at Leon who was reading a magazine. She knew him well. He had stood over her in ritual, raped and beaten her. There was nothing nice about him. She shuddered as she recalled the conversation in the car on the way over here.

"You need to be careful, little lady. Sometimes it doesn't matter who your daddy is if the rules you break are big enough. You came close last night. Can't let that happen again, now can we. You know who gets into trouble if you talk?"

He looked at her, not really expecting an answer, but for emphasis. His cold eyes locked on hers, looking for her fear. He preyed on that fear. Alissa locked the fear out of her eyes and stared back at him, her own eyes cold.

"You're the one going down if you talk. The world will know what a whore you are and whores are thrown into jail and forgotten about. Don't forget, we got connections everywhere, even in jail. It's not like you'd be safe there. We can get to you there, and it'll all be over. Not like they'd do it quickly. Nice and slow, reminding you why. A whore and a rat. Not a good combination. So be careful. You hear me?"

Their eyes locked again, but only for a moment before Leon had to watch the road. Alissa vowed within her not to give him what he looked for. He wanted her to be afraid. He wanted to feel powerful. He wanted to take her power. She refused to give it to him. Somehow, despite his words, she knew this was not her destiny. It may be her present path, but it was not her destiny.

In the office, as they waited, she thought about what she believed her destiny was. Even at 8 she knew she was meant for great things. She wondered why she thought that as the door opened and a man in a white coat approached her.

"Hello, Leon. Who do you have for me today?"

"Hey, Doc. This is Alissa. Alissa Campbell. Name sound familiar? Just do what you need to so we can get her back to her family where she belongs."

Leon turned to Alissa, "Go with the doctor and do what he says. It's all for the best. You know that."

Alissa stood up and followed the doctor into the door. Her thoughts of Leon lasted only a few minutes as she entered a small room with a chair and funny wires running out from all angles.

"Need you to get up on that chair, my dear. The nurse will help you get out of your clothes and into a gown. This therapy will help you remember the things you seem to have forgotten. It might hurt a little but we all know, no pain no gain."

Alissa felt the fear in the pit of her stomach. She was in the chair with a nurse removing her clothes. Once naked, she was given a hospital gown and told to sit back in the chair. The angle of the chair tilted so far back Alissa could see the ceiling. Her head, arms, legs and waist were strapped to the chair. The fear rose inside her. She tried to counter the fear with that sense of knowing, but couldn't. As the wires were glued to her head, arms and torso, she began to slip away. She was not fast enough as she felt the first surge of the shock therapy. But it was short lived. She was in her Sacred Place.

"Doctor, I don't know what happened to her. She seems to have lost consciousness. It was just the first jolt. We've not had that happen before."

"It's alright, nurse. Let me have a look."

He bent over the child. "Alissa, can you hear me?"

The child stirred. Slowly her eyes opened. She didn't know where she was. She didn't know who she was. She was afraid. She couldn't move. Wires were everywhere. What was happening? She looked at the man towering over her, a man in a white coat with no hair and a gray beard. Who was he? Why was she here?

"It's okay, Nurse. She's back with us. Let's try again."

He slipped away out of sight. The child didn't know what to think. She had been in a safe, warm place a few minutes before, deep inside in the Sacred Place. Now she was here. Alissa had left again. Sadie knew it was her turn to bear the burden. But she didn't know what the burden was. Then she felt the shock, the electricity pulsed through her. She screamed.

"Hey, no noise! It's not that bad. We've done this before. Lay back and relax. You know the routine. Nurse, start the light pattern. That's good."

The lights, red and blue, pulsed on and off, alternately. Additionally, the rules of The Organization played quietly, a deep voice reiterating with threatening reverberation.

"Okay, the machine is set. Let's leave it for now."

The two left the room as another shock shot through the young body, causing muscles to contract and a whimper to pass her lips.

"No noise. No tears. No tell. Do what you're told. Ask no questions. Secrets are sacred. Evil lives within you. You are bad. If you tell, the world will know you are bad and will punish you..."

The tirade on the tape continued as the child slipped in and out of consciousness. Sadie fought off another trying to take over the body. She could feel the evil in the other. Her job was to protect the body, to ensure their survival. This other, created from the electric machine, threatened that survival. It was hard to fight that and feel the pain of the electric shocks. But she had no choice.

Sadie cried out to the Ancestors, for someone to help her. She felt strength as another from the Sacred Place joined her in the fight. Together they took the evil one and put him in the place inside just past the mountains where the other Dark Ones lived. Here the Dark Ones could be contained, kept inside, just at the edge of the Sacred Place. It was true that the Evil Ones on the outside could call them out to do their bidding, but The Troops within, those who inhabited the Sacred Place, had found a way to protect themselves from the Dark Ones.

Chapter 14: Inside, Outside...

Sadie knew well the inside world. The Sacred Place, created by Alissa to provide safety from a horrific existence, was a beautiful place. Those who lived there, created to take on that horrific existence when Alissa could not, were called The Troops. None of them was older than the body. Each was the age of their creation. The youngest among them, 10-month-old Lena, was really the oldest for she had been created first, when the body was 10 months old.

The Troops had a rank and file, with each member having a job. Some knew how to withstand severe pain. Others knew the rules of certain games well and came to play them with the perpetrators. Still others knew the words to say when the question and answer sessions took place. And so on, each one knowing when to take their place.

Alissa had created the Sacred Place, knowing well when she went there. She had little thought for the outside world and what happened when she retreated within. The Troops were the creation to fill that void. When Alissa slipped away, someone else had to ensure the survival of the body. That was the driving force in all of them; survival, at all costs and above all else. It was their universal truth. Alissa knew that there were friends and playmates within, but her consciousness would not allow her to confront who they really were or what they really did. She chose her oblivion as a method of survival. Subconsciously she created this inside world to provide herself a place to retreat and tactical war plan to survive. It was all one neat package in a single body with a single purpose.

Some within knew and recognized others well. There were others that knew no one else. These were sad and lonely children for they stayed in their single Safe Place and touched no one else, the horrors and secrets they held so devastating they had trouble containing it themselves. Their jobs were to hold those secrets, too great for any one person to know and survive, so that Alissa could survive. Everyone accepted their roles without question and sought to protect Alissa from the truths they held. For Alissa, ignorance was bliss.

Those like Speed and Sadie did their jobs effectively. But when Alissa did return, it was often disorienting to her. She had lost the time when the others were in the body. She had no idea what had happened, where she had been or how she behaved. The others could compensate for some of that and worked to feed her enough information so she could squeak by, not appearing too out of it. Drawing attention to themselves was not what they wanted. Quite the opposite. Just being was their goal. It was how survival was guaranteed.

So, when the worlds collided, when Alissa found herself disoriented, there had to be some quick action to correct itself. Using dreams and Alissa's time in the Sacred Place, they worked to provide enough continuity to life that appearances caused little wonder for the outside world. Slowly, Alissa came to accept the disorientation as normal and followed her gut to guide her through. She did very little thinking about it and never spoke of it to anyone.

Outside, there were some discrepancies. But with the life she led, few noticed. There were no questions about the obvious. Who would question the subtle? And so it was that Alissa created for herself a survival tool within her to survive the unsurvivable.

The Sacred Place gave her sanctuary. It was a place to go that guaranteed emotional peace. The Troops gave her survival. They took on the abuse, the trauma, the damage and feelings. They guaranteed the body would survive. Together, The Troops and the Sacred Place protected the Spirit of Laughing Star, Mama's child. That was their job.

Outside was often a nightmare. When Alissa was not in her Sacred Place, she was high. It was how she made it work. It was how she followed the rules. In the outside world, sleep meant nightmares at the very least. At the very worst, it meant a visit from someone. Sometimes it was her father. Other times it was someone sent to her who had paid to use her for the night.

Inside was always peaceful and wonderful. Here sleep was gentle and safe. The feelings of the wind and breezes often seemed to carry songs she vaguely remembered from somewhere deep inside. She couldn't hear the words, couldn't remember them. But she listened and felt the comfort in the melodies, somehow knowing someone, beyond herself, was watching over her, keeping her safe.

Over time, Alissa spent more and more time inside. The Troops grew in numbers, developing those who had the skills necessary to take on, not just the abuse and terror, but everyday life. Some went to school and learned and played. Others established themselves within the neighborhood, again ensuring their survival on yet another domain. Some were domestic and organized. Once created, the individual grew in what they could do, what they liked, how they acted. "Alissa," on the outside, took on a multitude of talents and abilities, honed by inside individuals and manifested as one on the outside. She was smart, physically active in sports, strong-willed, a bully who defended the underdog, a drug dealer and addict… multi-faceted. The people in the outside world that were not her abusers, loved and admired her. As a whole, she had mastered living. But there was a price to pay.

From within, Alissa lost track of the outside world. She slipped further and further away, aware of the outside and participating at a very peripheral level. It was as if she watched herself doing life. She had no desire to be a part of it, but liked to check in and see how things were progressing. It was more like a movie experience that she could view but then could easily slip back to her comfort and protection within.

But she survived. That was the objective.

Chapter 15: The Thug…

Eris was a member of The Troops. Her job was to manage the outside dark world for Alissa. That meant, by and large, she was the thug. At 9 years old she had been taught well to pick locks. As it turned out, she had a knack for it. There were few locks she couldn't break. So, three nights a week she and her crew went out in the rich neighborhoods, looking for goods. Her crew consisted of herself and her cousins, Tammy and Johnny, and her half brother, J. R. The way it went down was for Eris to get them in, J.R. was the lookout, and Tammy and Johnny ransacked the place. The goal was not to turn the place upside down. They identified specific targets, having been informed by the boss back at the shop what they were looking for. Some nights it was only a specific line of stereos. Other nights there was an order for a specific television or other electronic device. Occasionally, they had the opportunity to go after something really valuable; jewelry or money. In exchange, the four of them got their stash for the week.

It seemed to Eris to be a sweet deal. Three nights a week, guaranteed no abuse or ritual, and she walked away with enough cocaine to keep her happy for the whole week. Who could ask for anything more?

Eris carried herself well at school and in the neighborhood, her demeanor assuring all those around her that she could and would take care of herself. She was well known to throw down without much thought about where or when and accepted the consequences,

if caught, with little remorse. Somehow teachers and adults in her world still liked her. She was a good student even if she had a questionable attitude. Those who understood the neighborhood and the cost of growing up and staying alive here knew why Eris behaved the way she did.

But Eris had a weak point. She hated to see anyone targeted for being different or appearing "weak." She was the self-appointed defender of the underdog. Not that she announced that to anyone. But she believed in the concept of a fair fight. Six-on-one was seldom fair odds. Those who did not have the skills and talents for the streets still had to go to school and had a right to live their lives. Eris felt it was her job to make sure that was the case. So she ended up with an interesting mingle of friends.

Interestingly enough, Eris also always had a smile for the world. No matter who you were, friend or foe, Eris met you with a smile. The eyes might give her away; sometimes taunting, sometimes inviting, always gleaming. Living was what Eris was about. Surviving was her job. She just did it with style. The thug with style, that was Eris!

The Full moon weekend was approaching. Recently 9 and a half, Eris knew her rite of passage awaited. She hoped she had what it took to survive it. Within her, she knew if she couldn't do it, someone else from inside would. There was comfort in that.

There was no formal preparation for the event. No one even mentioned it. Eris just knew, like she knew the rules of The Organization, that it was time. She had watched others before her experience the same thing. There were others, also 9, who would face the same fate at the same time. Not all of them would make it alive. Eris was sure she would be one who did. Arrogance? No. Promise.

Eris knew, through the Littles within, who Mama was. She knew Little Red Feather and Silent Stone Beside the Water and tiny Mi-ca. She remembered who Laughing Star was and from whence she came. When Mama had crossed over, she had told Laughing Star that she must survive, that her existence would have the power to change the tides. No matter what it took, Laughing Star was to survive. That was Mama's final promise. And so it was. And so it would be.

"Alissa. Alissa!"

The voice was urgent as it shook her awake.

"It's time to get up, honey. Time for school."

Alissa's whole body ached. It had been a rough weekend. But she had survived. She wasn't sure how. But she attributed that to too much alcohol and too much high. Oh well. How else was she supposed to get through it? She was pretty sure she didn't want to remember it.

Moving from the side of the bed to stand, she fell to the floor. Her leg wouldn't hold her. The pain that burned up it screamed to be recognized.

"Mom! Help!"

Lori came in. "What's wrong, honey?"

"I think I broke my leg."

"Oh dear. Let me see. Yeah, it's pretty swollen. Let me get an ace wrap."

She disappeared out the door. Gram came to the door.

"I'll get you an aspirin for the pain."

Alissa would have preferred a little cocaine or a barby.

"Here, let me wrap that up and let's see if we can't get you on your feet."

Her mom wrapped the ankle tightly, with some level of expertise. Alissa was impressed.

"There. Try standing on that."

Alissa stood up. It would hold her to stand. She took a step and felt it give. It was not going to hold to walk.

"Okay. Let me call Dr. B. and see what he wants to do."

She disappeared out the door as Gram came in with two aspirin and a glass of water.

"Here, dear. This'll help a little. Why don't you sit back on the bed? We'll get it all taken care of."

Alissa sat down on the bed. What had happened? She decided she really didn't want to know and began to formulate her own story of what happened to give to the doctor. Her mom came in as she was firming up the story in her mind.

"Dr. B. says we might as well take you over to the Emergency Room and have it x-rayed. They can call him with the results right away and we can take care of it from there. I tell you, Alissa. You have more bumps, bruises and broken bones than anyone I know."

Alissa thought of the irony of that statement. She shook her head, not wanting to confront the lack of truth before her.

"Mom, today is our first baseball game! The third graders are taking on the fourth graders. I have to be there! I'm the short stop!"

"Exactly what do you think you're gonna be able to do? You can't even walk out of your own room! I know you want to be there. Maybe Gram can run you over to watch after everything gets taken care of. I have to get to work. Call if you need anything. Bye."

Alissa sighed in disgust. She didn't like it when such things got in her way. Especially when she wasn't even sure what happened in the first place!

"Come on, honey. I've got the car in the driveway."

Gram stood beside Alissa and helped her limp to the car. All the way to the hospital, Alissa was lost in her own thoughts. She had come to accept not knowing things. She expected it as part of the drug and alcohol use. At 9 years old, her habits were pretty heavy. But so were most of the kids around her. She wasn't that unusual.

Chapter 16: Life Passed On...

Eris had a cast on her left foot up to her knee, but it didn't stop her from doing too much. She couldn't run or move as quickly as usual, but she could still pick a lock and she could definitely throw a punch.

It was lunchtime and the line was too long. Eris was busy bullying her way closer to the front of the line when she suddenly didn't feel too good. The nausea quickly overtook her and she had to hobble as fast as she could to the girls' bathroom. Once there, she threw up until it was just dry heaves. When she felt better, she splashed a little water on her face, rinsed out her mouth and headed to the office.

"I'm sick. I need to go home."

"Nurses office is in the back. Go see her."

"Okay."

She walked to the back of the office. The nurse looked up from her paperwork, caught a glimpse of Eris and was on her feet.

"You don't look so good, little lady. Have a seat."

"I threw up in the bathroom. I think I need to go home."

"Been a rough week for you, hasn't it?"

"I guess. Can you call my grandmother, please?"

"Sure, hon. You just lie down here and I'll see if I can get her on the phone."

Gram came to pick her up within the hour. She could tell by looking at the child that she was not feeling well.

"I called Dr. B. He's expecting us at his office. Figured with everything else it wouldn't hurt for him to look you over."

Eris was too sick to care. She just went where she was led.

THE RED RUNS DEEP

"Can't find much wrong with her. No fever. No swollen glands. Might just be a reaction to the excitement of that fracture. Not that that's anything new to her. Take her home, put her to bed and let her rest. Best thing for her."

So that's what Gram did. She brought Eris some broth and crackers and set her up with a book and some yarn.

"Want me to teach you how to crochet?"

"Okay!"

There were times like these when Gram took extra time to teach her granddaughter some of the things her daughter had not wanted to be a part of. Alissa, as Gram knew her, enjoyed crocheting and sewing and learning how to do new things with her hands. Gram also enjoyed the closeness she felt with Alissa at these special times. She knew life for the child was far from easy. The bruises and injuries had not escaped her eye, she had just been severely warned not to notice. That was a long time ago, when Lori was still her daughter.

Lori had met Chuck shortly after he came out of the Marines. She told her mother she was in love. What her mother saw was not love but slavery. Chuck began to tell Lori what she could and could not do, say, wear or go. When the mother confronted her daughter, Lori told her to mind her own business. That night, two large men in dark coats and masks had broken into their home and threatened the older woman, telling her to ask no questions and remain silent or they would be back to bestow retribution.

Not one to challenge authority, Gram had fallen to silence. The price had also been the relationship between her and Lori. They grew distant until one day when Lori came to her and told her she hated her and never wanted to see her again. Hurting and confused, Gram didn't know what to do but to accept it. When Lori had come to her after leaving Chuck, Gram had thought there would be opportunity to mend their bond, to reunite as mother and daughter. Lori kept herself so busy that wasn't possible. She allowed Chuck to have Alissa so much that a relationship with the child was barely possible. Gram tried to make up for it when she could, such as moments like this.

"How would you like to go to church with us this Sunday," Gram asked Alissa.

"I'm with Dad on the weekends."

"What if I talked to your mom and maybe just this once you could be here this weekend? Would you like that?"

Alissa smiled, "Yes, I would."

"Let me see what I can do.

It was the middle of the night. It was dark. Eris felt a pain within her she couldn't identify. It was as if her insides were going to explode. She had thrown up everyday for a week. But just once a day. Tonight, the pain was a stabbing, burning pain she didn't know what to do with.

She looked to the bed next to her. Her mother wasn't there. Doubled over in pain, hobbling on her casted leg, Eris made her way to the hallway. There was a light in the living room.

"Mom! Gram!"

Gram reached her first.

"What's wrong, honey?"

"It hurts. Oh it hurts! My stomach. It hurts!"

"Lori, get the car. She needs to go to the Emergency Room."

"Okay, Mom, but you stay here. I can take her myself. You need to get your rest. You've spent enough time on her lately. I can take her."

Her tone confused, Gram responded, "Okay." To Alissa she said, "Let's get your coat and get you ready to go."

Once in the car, Eris knew Mom was not taking her to the Emergency Room.

"Where're we going?"

"Don't worry. Marge'll know what to do. Just sit there and be quiet. You're sick, remember?"

There was ice in her mother's voice. Eris wasn't sure why. What had she done wrong now? She felt the worlds change as she shifted to the Sacred Place and someone else came out to deal with the outside for a while.

Lauren took Eris' place in the outside world. She looked at Lori. Their eyes met. Lauren knew she should look away, but she just wanted to challenge the wench a little.

"When we get to Marge's you stay quiet. I'll explain everything. You know the rules. Keep your mouth shut. Don't speak unless spoken to. No noise. No tears. No tell."

"Yeah, I know the rules." Lauren felt something stab inside her, then she felt a rush out her vagina, as if she were peeing herself.

"I think something is wrong. I might have just pissed all over."

Upon inspection, blood was what Lauren felt spilling out of her. Lori had her pack it off with a few napkins and paper towels that were in the car. "We'll be there in a few minutes. Don't panic."

Lauren wasn't prone to panic. She had seen her own blood spilled all over the place before and lived to tell about it. By and large, she didn't feel the pain. It was a little uncomfortable at times, but it didn't hurt.

Lori drove, eyes forward, making no small talk, no eye contact. She just drove as if in a daze. She knew that Marge would know what to do. Chuck trusted the woman for everything. Hell, he would have taken Alissa to her for that broken leg. Marge probably would chastise her for going somewhere else. They did live a ways away from her. The hospital had been closer. The story Alissa recited about getting in a fight over the weekend seemed to satisfy the vultures in the ER. There were no questions and no inquiries. Lori figured she had done well with the situation.

They pulled into the driveway. Lauren saw the house she had known for so long. Nothing good ever happened here. It was just a place of silent pain. There were many buried here, a lot of blood spilled into the ground. She wondered if anyone really cared about all that. The Organization seemed to go on untouched, regardless of their deeds.

Lori was pulling Lauren out of the car now, up the walk. The cast slowed Lauren down a bit and that seemed to irritate Lori. *Good, let the bitch sweat it out,* Lauren thought to herself. She hated Lori, hated that she had to call her mom. She wasn't. Lauren knew that. Others

inside may have forgotten, but Lauren had not. She had been doing this for a while. Her job had begun at the age of 3, before Mama was gone.

As she limped up the steps, Marge came out and took her arm, helping her up.

"Girl, you are a mess. What's wrong that brings this child to Angel Marge's?"

"Bad stomach cramps and she's bleeding from her pussy."

"Hm. Can't be good. Get in here, let me take a look."

That could be scary all by itself. Marge frequently looked under the hood of the young girls. Most of the time she was checking for damage. But Lauren swore there were times Marge was between her legs for Marge's pleasure. Not that anyone would have cared. Lauren just didn't trust the woman. She climbed up on the exam table, already stripped of her pants.

"Lay back. I'll be gentle."

Lauren laid back, feet up in the stirrups, knowing Marge didn't care one way or the other if it hurt. She felt Marge put something cold inside her. A few minutes of probing and prodding, then Marge stood up.

"This child's pregnant. Looks like a miscarriage. Need to do a D&C, clean up that mess so we don't have to deal with infection later. Lori, can you help me out here?"

"Me?" Lori looked a little incredulous.

"Yes, you."

"I don't think so. I might pass out if there's too much blood."

"Well, there ain't nobody else. So yer elected! Grab that bottle right there and go boil some water. After it cools for a minute, put it in the bottle. Bring to me along with the hot water bottle and the hose with the douche head. You got all that?"

Lori nodded, seeming relieved that she would be away from the exam room.

"Okay, Alissa. You gonna hurt a bit, but you'll get over it. I think this yer first time. Might as well get used to it. Pretty standard procedure 'round here."

Marge stood up and walked to the cabinet, took out a syringe and walked out of the room.

From the other room she said, "I'll get you somethin' make this whole thing a little easier to take. You won't remember nothin'. Better that way."

She walked back in, the syringe full and a rubber strap in her hand. She tied the strap around Lauren's upper arm, tapped the inside of her elbow a couple times and stuck the needle in. Lauren was out of it before Marge had removed the strap.

Chapter 17: The Conflict Continues...

Over the last two years, Anastasia, one of The Troops, had become familiar with the church. Gram had insisted when Anastasia was 9 that she have at least one Sunday a month with her to go to church. Lori had tried to fight it, but eventually Gram won. Once a month turned into every other week. So it was that Anastasia went to church with her mom and Gram every other Sunday.

Sometimes the stretch between the worlds was tough. The Sundays she was not at church she was with her father, doing a lot of the things the church preached against. Anastasia decided she was probably not on God's good side. Her father told her she belonged to the Devil. Her mother swore she was Satan himself and most of the things Anastasia enjoyed were pretty well the same things that were going to end her up in hell.

Although she was only 11, Anastasia knew she was a victim to her father's tyranny, that The Organization owned her like it owned all those around her. She was forced to engage in sex and illegal activities, to offer herself and her actions in ritual to the Devil. She enjoyed the drugs and stealing, and fought daily in school to keep her name and reputation.

Yet, every other Sunday she sat in church and said all the right words in all the right places, memorized everything she was ever asked to and proved as an overachiever among her classmates. She could recite the books of the Bible, Old and New Testament. She

knew the familiar stories like the back of her hand and could recite many of them verbatim. She learned quickly how to engage in Biblical arguments and had enough Bible verses memorized to argue any angle. She became the bane of the pastor's existence since she worked hard to pose questions he couldn't answer and baited him with verses taken out of context.

She was seen among the church members as a smart young woman who knew her faith and was solid in her convictions. She became a pillar within the youth of the congregation.

Lori, too, became an important member of the church. She had the opportunity to go every Sunday and used that time to develop relationships with members of the congregation and their children. Before long, she was the leader of the youth group, planning and creating a variety of experiences for kids ages 9 and up. The members of the congregation saw her as a safe person for their children to be with, after all, her daughter was such a shining star.

Again, Anastasia's life was full of conflict. The Spirit that lived within her that believed in life as a sacred gift, the dark rituals she was forced to participate in with her father's world, and now this sugar coated concept of religion presented in her mother's world. As Alissa, she had no way to calm the conflict. Alissa just went inside to her Sacred Place and knew all would be well. The Troops were left to balance the worlds. Anastasia was part of that balance.

The best way such a balance could be achieved was to begin to create stronger barriers among the individuals inside. There were those whose purposes were everyday routines and activities; The Steadfasts. There were those whose jobs focused on withstanding the demonic rituals and the dark deeds; The Untouchables. These were different from the Dark Ones, created by the dark deeds, not a part of The Troops. There were still others who flourished in their work within the church; The Whites. There were those who lived as The Tribe Within The Troops, keeping alive the truths of the Ancestors, the gifts brought but not yet received. And there were those who knew of all the divisions, who oversaw The Troops as a whole, ensuring that no one violated the Law of Survival; The Captains.

So it came to be. Division began among them. There were those who shut out others. The Steadfasts turned blind to the others, except the Whites, whom they intermingled with. The Untouchables had little to do with anyone. They simply did their jobs and moved on, unaware that anything existed beyond the heinous pain and suffering they knew. The Tribe Within The Troops drifted to the mountains. If you listened closely at night, you might hear them drumming, but they were out of sight and out of mind. The Captains raced to keep the inside and outside world balanced. Continuity was important but not always smooth. Coping skills were taught from the inside, kibitzed into the consciousness.

The system within worked with its own consciousness, Alissa's sub-consciousness. The intricacies were created to mend the conflict she felt, to ensure she could survive the horror around her. There was an unspoken hope that someday the system that had been built to ensure her survival would also ensure her recovery. For now, she was shattered into many pieces.

Chapter 18: If It Doesn't Kill You...

Within The Organization, 12 years old was an adult. It was this time period that the expectations began to change. Up until now, the child was a victim, something to be manipulated and used, more like property than life. At 12, now the teaching began. The goal was to mold and develop a perpetrating machine that worked well. It was farewell to the victim, though the rules still applied. No noise, no tears, no tell.

And so, the rite of passage for 12 year olds was, physically, the most demanding. It was as if in saying goodbye to the victim, the perpetrators were going to inflict everything imaginable, and some things unimaginable, to test the strength and will of the child to survive. Perhaps it was some warped concept of the pains of labor, the trauma of birth. From child to adult.

Alissa was familiar with the intricacies that she had witnessed. There were many who had passed this milestone before her. As the youngest of the eight cousins, she had watched it happen in front of her. A few years before, she had seen her stepbrother, Charlie, Marge's son, die during his rite.

Death was a familiar face to Alissa. She didn't fear it. But she also knew she did not want to welcome it. That contradicted her very existence. The lurching threat of this rite brought the idea of death as a possibility to the forefront of Alissa's brain. As a rule, she did not think about death as something that could happen. She did not

contemplate its next threat. Her life was filled with enough fear-filled realities that she chose not to confront that aspect except when faced with the pains of possible pending doom.

Recently, she had turned 12. By the full moon of the sixth month after, she would journey to her rite of passage. It's not like it was optional. There were no choices. It would happen. Her ability to survive the rite would then give her the privilege to live on, tenuously. Her survival would mean those around her would try to cultivate within her a beast that could prey on the weak and enjoy it. Alissa knew no such beast dwelled within her. But for right now, she just needed to focus on surviving. One step at a time.

"Your father called. He wanted t' know if ya want to go horseback ridin'."

Now that was unusual. Alissa couldn't remember the last time her father called to ask her if she wanted to do anything, fun or otherwise. She had some vague recollection of a time when her father had his own racehorses, when he would sometimes take her to see them. But that was a long time ago and it had been years since he had sold off his horses and stuck simply to betting on their noses.

Yet, Alissa also longed to have a daddy that loved her, for whom she was good enough. She was his flesh and blood. Maybe now that she was growing up he was realizing what he had missed and wanted to act as her father instead of her pimp. Her heart hoped.

"Yeah! When does he want to go?"

"He says he'll pick ya up this weekend. It's not his normal weekend, but he wanted t' know if it'd be okay to have you anyway. You know, the horseback ridin' and all."

"Sure. Sounds great."

Alissa didn't think much more about it that Thursday afternoon. It was not until she noticed the night sky that her heart sank to her stomach. This was the full moon weekend. It was six months after her birthday. He was simply laying the groundwork to ensure he could have her when he needed her. There would be no horses ridden. She would be the only thing ridden this weekend. She dropped her head

to her hands. She might have cried if she knew how. But the tears had long been beaten out of her. Instead, her heart beat hard against her chest and her mind raced with the fears of what lay ahead. Clenching her fists to her eyes, she went to her Sacred Place.

It was the Monday after. Dad was dropping her off at school. She had done the best she could to cover most of the bruises and marks. The hardest part was not limping on her right leg. One of the bones had been snapped Saturday night. She knew because she heard it. But until the softball game tonight, she couldn't limp. There, within the first inning or two, she would find a way to feign an injury so she could get the medical treatment she needed. There were those who said it was impossible to walk on such a bad break. As one of The Troops, Tess had learned it really was about mind over body. You moved the pain into the palm of your right hand. There you could hold it, clench it and keep it from taking over the brain.

That meant as she got out of the dirty Cadillac she held her right fist near her pants pocket, looking like it was supposed to be there. She was tired and grumpy and she looked it. That was good. People would leave her alone.

She had enough of a reputation at school that most of the kids didn't mess with her. It's not that she won every fight she was ever in. She had definitely gotten her ass kicked more than once. But she put up a hell of a fight in the meantime and did her own level of damage. Some of it was credit to the abuse she had known for so long. It took most people quite awhile of wailin' on her to get her to the point where she felt it or it had impact enough to slow her down. That's how she got their respect. Not by always winning, but by always persevering. Hardheaded instigator, true. But no one would call her mean.

Today, she walked slowly. Hey! She was tired! And she sat down a lot. But hey! She was tired! No one gave her much lip. She slept through most of her classes and ignored people by and large. As the last bell rang, she headed to the locker room to change and then out to the field. She passed the ball back and forth with a couple of the

other players. Then she sat on the bench with a water bottle in her hand and waited.

Coach talked to the girls, "Blah, blah, blah."

Umpires talked to the teams, "Blah, blah, blah."

Teams did their little pep circle, "Rah, rah, rah."

And the game began. As the short stop, Tess knew she would get action soon enough to be able to get off her feet. Of course, just her luck, the pitcher was having a great game and struck out the first batter, didn't even get a tip off.

Next batter. Swing and a strike. Two balls. At last, a hit! Right down the first base line. The infield threw the ball around, just to stay loose.

Ball is back to the pitcher. Two strikes, two balls. Pitcher needs to throw a sweet pitch. A swing and a miss. Batter out. Great. Two batters struck out. Tess wasn't sure she could actually bat and run the bases. She'd have to try at this rate.

Third batter. Big girl. Pitcher squares off and let's go with a curve. The batter half swings, pulls up. Ball. Second pitch, the batter takes a back step, swings and connects solid on the meat of the bat. The ball heads into the air. Tess judges it to land just behind her and in front of the sweeper. She heads for the ball, noticing the sweeper is coming to the ball, as well. As Tess collides with the other player, she goes down hard on her right leg. The ball plops near them. The sweeper picks it up and throws it to the second baseman to prevent the runner from advancing. Tess lays holding her leg, waiting for her coach to come out to the field. Relief floods over her.

As she lay on the gurney in the hospital, Tess recounts the last few days. She has survived. Little else matters today. She is counting her blessings as the doctor approaches.

"That's a really nasty break. Looks like it's going to require a little surgery to set it so it heals correctly. Your mother is on her way down now. We'll talk more when she gets here, okay?"

Tess isn't sure what that means exactly. Usually a broken bone means they might have to tug and pull a little to set it, might even

have to knock her out so they can manipulate it a bit more, but never surgery. What will Dargon have to say about it?

Worry racing, Tess slips away. Another comes to take her place. Nancy is brand new at this. Her existence began this weekend. She is unfamiliar with what she sees around her. The white is a contrast she cannot decipher. People around her are talking to her like they know her, yet she doesn't recognize any of them. She stares at them, not knowing what to say. It's obvious that was not the right thing to do.

"'lissa. You a' right? You sure is actin' weird."

The young girl to Nancy's right is looking at Nancy like she is supposed to say something. She wonders what she should do, what she should say. Having no exposure to societal norms, Nancy is unsure how to respond to a question about her well-being. All she knows is those who could care less, those who set out to harm and destroy her. Surely this must be a ploy to make her vulnerable.

"Maybe the doc needs to check out yer head. Musta hit dat, too."

There is laughter at the remark from the boy just in front of Nancy.

As she looks around, she realizes people surround her. She feels panic rise in her throat. All she can do is scream. Not a blood-curdling scream of fear. She hears herself screaming, "Get off of me! Get away! Don't touch me! No! Stop! Get off!"

The crowd scatters a bit as a man in a white coat steps through. Reaching for her, his words trying to calm her, he terrifies her even more. She lunges at him, continuing the screaming and ranting. She thrashes and throws herself at anyone and anything that moves. Like a cornered animal, her terror rises and her defenses mount.

"Get the restraints. Get me a sedative. Call for a CT scan. I might've missed a head injury," the doctor is calling over his shoulder while trying to calm Nancy at the same time.

"It's okay, honey. Little too much excitement," over his shoulder he yells, "Can someone get these people outta here, please?"

"Okay, folks. You heard the man, let's move it into the waiting room. The little lady is just a bit shook up. We'll let the doctor take care of her. Come on now."

A man in green scrubs moves the mass of bodies out of the ER and

into the waiting room. In the meantime, Nancy's panic is escalating.

The nurse has brought an injectable sedative to the doctor. Nancy, fearing the needle, increases her raging and attempts to run from the room. As she stands, the injured leg, not yet splinted or casted, gives way and she falls to the floor. The doctor takes the opportunity to inject the narcotic as he helps Nancy to her feet.

"Okay, Alissa. Let's get you back on the bed."

"My name is Nancy," she starts to say, but the meds have hit and she loses control of her mouth and tongue. As she falls the nurses lift her to the bed.

"Put soft restraints on her. I'm not sure what's going on, but I don't want a repeat."

Nancy drifts off to sleep.

Chapter 19: Sanity, Sanity...

"You have to understand, Mrs. Campbell, we're concerned for Alissa's safety. We have set and casted her leg. But she has a significant head injury and several other contusions and abrasions. We'd like her to stay one more night."

"You've had her three days already. Just tell me what she needs and I'll make sure she gets it when we get 'er home."

"We can't guarantee she won't experience another episode like she had in the ER. We've had a couple unusual occurrences on the floor, as well. We'd like to make sure that the phenomenon we're seeing dissipates before we release her."

"I understand, Doctor, but don't you think she'd be better off healin' at home? My mom don't work, so she can stay with her. We'll make sure she's not alone."

"There are some discrepancies as well, Mrs. Campbell."

"What d' you mean?"

"Some of the injuries are not injuries we would expect to see based on the account of the incident that brought Alissa to the hospital."

"It's a rough town, Doctor. She pro'bly got herself into a scuffle at school or before the game. I'm sure she can explain it for us later."

"I'm afraid I'm going to have to insist, ma'am. I've already placed a hold on her that allows me to keep her here until Child Welfare completes an investigation."

"What?"

"I have to act in Alissa's best interest. I have concerns and I want to be absolutely sure everything is all right before she goes home. Our Social Work department will work with you and the Agency to get this matter taken care of as quickly as possible."

"Well, I… How could you? She's my daughter, my only flesh and blood. How could you?" Lori stood up, almost threatening, tears in her eyes.

"I'm sorry." Into the phone he said, "Get me security, please."

"I just want my baby."

"I understand. Now if you'll go with these gentlemen, they'll escort you to the lobby where you can wait for our Social Worker to come talk with you. I'll phone her now and have her come right down."

The two security officers each took an arm, escorting the woman out of the doctor's office. Lori just shook her head, dazed. She allowed the men to walk her to the lobby. Looking around she spotted a pay phone.

"Chuck? It's me. The hospital won't release Alissa, somethin' 'bout a hold until Child Welfare completes an investigation. We can't have that. Whada I do?"

She paused, listening.

"Okay. Uh huh. You sure? Okay, I trust ya. Thanks. Bye."

She hung up the phone. A young woman entered the lobby and looked her way. "Mrs. Campbell?"

"Yes."

"My name is Kim and I'm the hospital Social Worker. You want to come upstairs and we'll see if we can get this under way?"

Lori went with the woman, unsure of what it all meant, but quite confident Chuck would take care of it.

"Hello, again, young lady." Leon approached Alissa in her hospital room.

Alissa looked at him with blank eyes, as if she didn't recognize him.

"Who're you?" she asked.

"My name is Leon. I'm here to talk to you a little bit. What's your name?"

"Brindle."

"Hi, Brindle. Will you talk to me?"

"Maybe."

"What are you doing here, Brindle?"

"Just watching."

"What?"

"Just watching."

"Oh. I thought your name was Alissa."

"Oh, yeah. It is."

"And what are you doing?"

"Waiting."

"Waiting for what?"

"I don't know."

"So, how will you know when it happens?"

"Someone will know."

"Okay. What if I told you, you could go home with your mom today?"

"Huh?"

"Would you like to go home with your mom today?"

"If you say so."

"I say so. Don't forget the rules when you go places, okay?"

"What rules?"

"No noise. No tears. No tell."

"I remember."

"Good."

"What do you mean the investigation is completed?" The doctor was on the phone and he wasn't happy. The nurse hung back at the door.

"You just started the investigation yesterday. Yeah. You found no indicators that caused you any concern? Okay. Then my hands are tied. I'll send her home."

He hung up the phone, "I can't believe it!"

"What's that, Dr. Miller?

"Child Welfare didn't find anything unusual with the Campbell case. Our staff certainly did. The child acted like she was terrified most of the time. The rest of the time it was as if she was only 2 or 3 years old. Go figure."

"I know, Doctor. Sometimes it's hard to understand how things happen."

"Maybe the kid's just crazy. She certainly acted odd. If there was nothing wrong with the family, then maybe it's the kid."

"Not our problem, sir. Let it go. You have a full roster today."

"Yeah, you're right."

Brindle was two. She was part of The Troops. She had been stuck out for almost four days now. She didn't know why and she didn't know what to do. All she could do was wait. It was scary out here in a body that was too big. She had owwies and a big, heavy sock on her foot. She didn't like it. The ladies in white at the other place had been nice to her. She got ice cream and they patted her on her head. The mommy-lady came to see her just once while she was there. She yelled at Brindle to "grow up." Brindle thought about that and wondered what that meant and how she could do that. Back here, at the house, the Grammie-lady was mostly nice to her, too. She looked at Brindle funny sometimes, but brought Brindle a color book and colors and let her watch 'toons on the box. It was fun. Then the mommy-lady came home.

"All right, brat. You got some explainin' to do. What the hell do you think yer doin' pullin' shit like that at the hospital? Do ya know how much grief and worry ya caused me? I'm fixin' to whip your bare ass 'cuz I know you can't run away!"

Brindle didn't like that. She was afraid of the whipping. She didn't know what to say. She just sat there, hoping the mommy-lady would just go away.

"What, ya got nothin' to say? Well, I'll jus' go get the strap and we'll see what ya got t' say after that!"

Lori walked to the bedroom and opened the top drawer. She took

out the strap she kept rolled there for just such an occasion. How could the child think she could get away with this? Chuck was gonna kill her!

"All right. Here I come. Get yer pants to yer ankles and bare up that ass. You got a whippin' comin' like you ain't never had from me before."

Brindle just sat there. She didn't know what to do. She was afraid; afraid to talk, afraid to move, afraid of what was going to happen. She knew she couldn't win at this point. She just wished someone would come and save her.

Lori was already angry and to see Alissa sitting on the couch, not moving despite the directions she was given just made her more angry.

"You little piece of shit."

The belt just started falling. Brindle couldn't get out of the way of it and felt it hitting her on her face, chest, stomach, back, legs... anywhere Lori could reach. The little one started screaming. Gram came running.

"Lori Renee, what are you doing to that child? Stop it!"

"Oh, get off your high horse, Mom, like you never whipped me! Or her for that matter!"

Gram backed off at the harsh words. Her daughter was right. What right did she have to correct her? Besides Alissa was her daughter. Maybe Lori would do better than she had. She walked away, hearing the cries and screams of her granddaughter.

Brindle slipped away to the inside. Tess reclaimed the outside and grabbed her mother's arm.

"Stop it, bitch or I'll break your arm!"

"Oh, now you can talk to me! What the hell is going on?"

The belt lay limp in Lori's hand now, Tess having a hold at the wrist.

"I don't know but you better back off before I lose it with you."

"Oh yeah, like you can do anything about it. Now bare your ass and let me give you what you have coming. The quicker you get on with it, the quicker it gets over."

Tess glared at Lori. She also thought about it for a minute. She wasn't sure what was happening, but it wasn't anything good. Dargon was probably already going to make her regret what she didn't know and anything more was only going to make it worse. It wasn't like Tess couldn't take Lori. She was stronger and faster and she carried a switchblade and had access to guns. But, and it was a big but, Dargon was a scary man. Anything Tess did to Lori Dargon was sure to know about and make sure she paid for. In the end, it was easier to take the whipping from Lori and let it go, hoping Dargon had bigger issues to deal with the next time she saw him. She could only hope.

As Lori took out the last of her rage on Tess' backside, Tess sought for answers on what had happened. It seemed that The Troops were losing their grip on the balance and life outside was a little unpredictable. When it was over, Tess laid on the couch, cast in the air, trying to keep too much pressure off the areas that took the brunt of the beating.

What was happening? They couldn't afford to lose control. It could be deadly. She closed her eyes, going inside, releasing the body to a dreamless sleep.

Chapter 20: No Even Odds...

Alissa was now 14 years old, a freshman. High school was a big change, not because Alissa wasn't ready academically or even socially. No, now she was one of the youngest, the freshest blood. The inner-city high school had a two-block radius called 'Survivor Island.' If you managed to get from that two block mark to the school building without being shot the first week of school, you had a pretty good chance at making it through the school year alive. Out of 463 freshmen, 21 didn't make it through the first month of high school. Not that they were all fatalities. Some parents transferred their kids to private school if they could. It was the beginning of desegregation and busing. There were racial tensions, turf tensions and clique tensions. Still, Alissa felt safer at school than at home.

Desegregation meant that the school that had been 100 percent non-white now became 20 percent white. As a Native American child, Alissa was still in the minority. Her grade school reputation helped, but she knew alone it wouldn't be enough. Then divine intervention stepped to the plate.

Kendall was a senior. He was 6 foot 4 inches tall at 285 pounds and it was all muscle. Somehow, he took a liking to Alissa. Not as a girlfriend or even a whore, more like a little sister. Alissa didn't know what it was that influenced the bond, but they clicked. She blessed it and called it good.

That friendship guaranteed few would mess with Alissa. Word traveled fast and everyone that mattered soon knew if they messed

with her they messed with Kendall. He was a leading member of The Kings, one of the toughest gangs on the street. Not too many people wanted to piss him off. It made Alissa's freshman year pretty comfortable.

Because of who her 'big brother' was, she had senior privileges. That meant she could sit in the senior lounge, smoke and toke with them and build a stronghold as the supplier for the senior class. It was all working out very well! A larger buyer line meant she kept her suppliers happy. If they were happy, she was happy. There was little more she could ask for. At school. Home was a different story. The expectations of Alissa as a willing participant and perpetrator were growing. And she was failing miserably. There was no one within The Troops that could tow the mark. The only way any of them could bring themselves to hurt another was through coercion.

So coerce they did. Many years ago, kittens had been used as examples of what might happen to someone who refused to do the bidding of The Organization. Many of the Littles had watched as kittens and cats were cut, sliced, strangled, drowned and tortured. It was an effective tool. Any of the Littles exposed to such tragedy became pretty compliant.

As age increased, the ante was upped. Now as The Organization sought to mold the beast that would perpetrate with relish, significant harm was threatened to smaller children should the perpetrator refuse. Most often it was a worse fate than the deed expected from the perpetrator.

So it was that Teri, the member of The Troops who was now out, stood naked before a 3-year-old boy, ordered to rape him. Lenny stood with a gun to the right side of her head.

"Do it or die, bitch."

She hesitated. It was a tough choice. Just the other day she had prayed to die, herself, at the hands of a sadistic john who wanted more than anything to see her bleed. Most of the clan you didn't look in the eye, but Lenny, well, he was different. He wasn't too bright. He was good at doing what he was told and little else. She locked his gaze on hers. She heard a hammer cock in her left ear. Uncle John stood to

her left. He was mean to the quick, not someone you challenged. She submitted to the directive.

Teri tried to talk to the child with her eyes, to convince him to cooperate and it would be over quickly. She was enveloped in his cries.

"He's breakin' the rules, what're ya gonna do about it, bitch?"

Teri did nothing. She felt a hand raise her by the hair and throw her backward.

"I said, he's breakin' the rules. Ya know we can't let dat happen."

That said, Uncle John began to beat the boy with his bare hands, yelling the rules over the child's screams. He didn't stop until the child lay silent and motionless. Teri could see he was still breathing. She wasn't sure if that was a good thing or not.

"You jus' don't get it, do ya, bitch?" He grabbed her hair and dragged her down beside the child. She fell limp and silent as he raged and raped her. There was nothing more she could do. His anger had to run its course. Better her than someone smaller.

The meeting had been called in the darkest of night, a moonless night. The topic of conversation was a member of The Organization who was trying to get out, trying to rat out the lot of them. The discussion was not determination of the member's guilt. That had already been determined. The true issue was what the punishment would be. Teri knew from the direction of the comments that she would play a key role. She didn't like that idea at all.

"Come with me."

Dargon did not look at her, just motioned in her direction.

"The talk in the circle is that you ain't yet proved yer worthy to stay alive. Tonight ya prove it. Follow directions. Exactly. Otherwise, you'll be next. Got it?"

Teri knew there was to be no answer. She understood clearly what was at stake. She hoped she had it in her to do what was required. There was always the backup of someone within The Troops, but she knew this was her job. It would require the creation of another within to take over if she failed. It would be better if that were not the case.

They were driving out through a dingy trailer park, all the way to the back. Someone shot out the streetlight in front of the third trailer from the end.

"Git up there and lock those two doors. Lean these two steel bars up against 'em so they can't bust out so easy. See that front window, it's the only one big enough to get through. Jim gonna lock his tommy on that one. You set fire to the back o' the place first, then throw the Molotov through the window. Got all dat?"

Teri looked at Uncle John in disbelief. They were going to burn the whole family inside the trailer, alive. She knew that the man in question had a wife and three young children. She just stared at the things he tried to hand her.

"Don' forgit. Dere's lots at stake for you tonight."

She took the things from him, numbly. She followed his instructions and then retreated to behind the car. She crouched low, afraid to watch. She heard an explosion, gunfire, a child scream and then an infant cry. She couldn't help herself. She turned around. Obviously, the young mother had tried to come through the window with the baby. She had been shot before she ever hit the ground. But the baby was still alive, squalling. No one else seemed to notice it. Before she realized what she was doing, she was sprinting toward the infant. She was beside the baby when a shot rang out. The tiny body exploded as she reached for it. Looking over her shoulder, Jimmy grinned at her. It was an ugly grin. It was then that Teri felt the heat from the blaze and was forced to back away.

They were all heading back to the cars and leaving. Sirens blared somewhere in the distance. Their job was done. They left. In the backseat, Teri stared blankly at her hands. They were singed and still had bits of blood and flesh from the infant. It was all she could do not to vomit where she sat. No matter how she thought about it, the odds were stacked against her. The question of survival entered her mind. What kind of survival was this? Lost in those thoughts, she drifted inside to the Sacred Place.

Chapter 21: Reality? Insanity?

"I'm worried. I can't even get her out of bed, Lori. She just stares up at the ceiling. Won't talk to me. Won't answer me. Nothin'."

Gram was on the phone with Lori. It was the second day in a row she couldn't get Alissa out of bed. It was as if the child was slipping away. Lori didn't seem to care or didn't know what to do, Gram wasn't sure which.

"What d'ya want me to do, Mom? I'm at work. Can't you just deal with her? Maybe she's sick or tired or... I don't know. Just deal with it."

There was a click. Lori had hung up. Gram wasn't sure what to do. She hung up the phone and went to the kitchen. She poured herself a cup of coffee and sat down. She just stared out the window, praying for some kind of guidance or a sign or something.

There was a crash from the living room. Gram sprang to her feet and raced to the origin of the sound. To her horror, Alissa had jumped through the plate glass window in the front room. She lay in the front flowerbed, crying, but not moving.

"Alissa, honey. Are you all right? What's got into you?"

"Don't wanna die. Don't wanna die. Don't wanna die. Don't wanna die."

The child was now sitting and rocking, surrounded by shattered glass, little trickles of blood falling from her face and upper arms. Gram came to her, trying to quickly assess if any of the cuts were serious. It didn't appear so. They all looked pretty superficial. But the child was obviously not doing well. A neighbor came running over, "I

117

called the police. Told them to send an ambulance. Anything else I can do?"

"Thanks, Agnes. Can you watch her for a minute? I'm going to get a blanket. I'll be right back."

"Sure. It's okay, honey. Agnes is here. Grandma's gonna go get you a blanket. There. There. It'll be okay."

The lights to the emergency vehicle came into view. "See, here come some nice people to help you."

The hospital room had two beds and two dressers in it. Nothing more. Teri had a roommate. Her walls had posters of teenage heartthrobs and self-created artwork. Teri sat on her white-sheeted bed, knees to her chest. She was dressed in her street clothes without shoes. The Emergency Room staff had admitted her to the Adolescent Psychiatric Ward as soon as they determined she had no serious injuries. Lori hadn't even gotten there yet. Gram was downstairs, lost in the paperwork maze, waiting for Lori to arrive.

"Rebecca, can you excuse us for a minute. I have to do some paperwork with your new roommate."

The nurse that came in could have been any Joe off the street. She didn't wear scrubs or white shoes. She wore a nametag that said "Michelle" but that was all.

The blonde-haired girl on the other bed nodded and smiled, "Sure thing. I'll be in the t.v. room."

"So, Alissa. I have some questions to ask you. You feeling up to answering?"

Teri just stared at her. It was sometimes hard to remember to answer to Alissa. That was the name the body went by, but when things were so fuzzy anyway, it was hard to remember.

"Does that mean no?" the nurse continued. "None of these are hard questions. How are you feeling?"

Teri couldn't feel anything. She just looked at the woman, trying to formulate a thought to express. She wasn't very successful.

"You're safe here. It's not a bad place. You'll be free to move around on the floor as you please. There's a T.V. room and a library

on the floor. You'll go to group therapy and art therapy and a couple times a week, in the evening, we go swimming. We have docs here to talk to, if you want, and we nurses are always willing to listen. Do you want to take a tour?"

Michelle extended a hand to Teri. Teri just looked from the hand to Michelle's face, trying hard to get her brain to cooperate.

"Okay. Well, maybe later. I'll let you rest. I'll send in an orderly with some meds to help you relax. Don't you worry about a thing."

Teri was alone in the room. She looked around. The door opened and a little man in scrubs with a syringe walked in.

"Got some meds for you."

Teri was gone in a flash and Nancy was in her place, screaming.

"Need a little help in here." The orderly didn't seem flustered or even surprised. The door opened and more people came into the room, more than Nancy could count. She screamed and fought, kicking and biting, until she felt her arms tied to the bed. Her screaming became blood-curdling as she saw her life flashing before her eyes, images of the nightmares she had lived flipping like a movie before her. She felt a stick in her hip and suddenly everything went dark.

"We finally have her resting, Mrs. Campbell. You'll have to wait to see her until later. Visiting hours begin at 6 PM."

"But she's my daughter. I want to see her, make sure she's all right. I left work for this!"

"I'm sorry. She's had a rough go of it. They had some trouble with her upstairs. She's sleeping now. She'll probably sleep through the afternoon, might even still be groggy this evening. I suggest you go home or back to work and come back later, during visiting hours."

"Lori, obviously there's nothing more we can do here. Let's go and we can maybe figure out what we're going to do next." Gram was trying to reason with a tearful mother. Her own heart was breaking, but Gram figured Lori probably had a better idea what was going on than she did. Gram hoped to talk with Lori and get some answers.

Defeated, Lori nodded to her mother and they walked out of the hospital. What was Chuck going to say about this? She shuddered at the thought.

Chapter 22: Adding Perpetrators...

Nancy awoke and it was dark. It was dark in the room and it was dark outside. She was tied to the bed, not tightly, but securely. She tugged half-heartedly at the restraints. There was movement in the bed across the room. Nancy froze. Who could that be? Friend or foe? She lay perfectly still, listening, straining to hear. All she heard was the sound of breathing, sleeping breathing. Whoever it was, she need not fear them... for now.

She lay staring at the ceiling, trying desperately to ascertain where she was and what was happening. It was quiet. That was not something she was accustomed to; there should be loud noise. Then a door opening broke the silence. A slit of light slithered in. She saw a shadow approaching her bed.

"Ah. I see you're finally awake. You seem calmer now. Do you think I can untie you and you'll be okay?"

The man smiled. Another unusual event. Nancy looked at him, searching for something familiar. There was nothing.

"So, if I untie you, can you stay calm? Can't be comfortable to sleep like that."

Nancy realized he was waiting for her to respond. Another oddity. No one had ever expected her to talk to them, even if they asked a question. She looked to her wrists, padded in the restraints, not being cut by belts or straps. She looked back to the man.

"I'll take that as a yes," he said as he began unfastening the cuffs.

"My name is Steve," he continued. "I'll be your nurse tonight. I understand your introductions got cut off abruptly today. Maybe in the morning I can acquaint you to your surroundings before I'm off shift. Okay?"

Nancy looked at his smiling face and smiled herself. She nodded, careful not to make eye contact.

"Do you need anything else tonight?"

Nancy searched the floor, not sure how to answer. She had never used her voice for anything but screaming. She was created during the twelve-year rite of passage. Her only experiences were those that required her silence or her panic, nothing more. This situation was new. She wasn't sure what to do. Closing her eyes, she slipped back inside to the Sacred Place.

Tess had no idea where she was or what was going on. The man standing over her as she lay in a hospital bed seemed to be waiting for something. She looked at him, trying to determine how to react.

"What?" was all she could muster.

"I asked if you needed anything else tonight. You have a bathroom here in your room that you are free to use as you need or want. There's a shower, but no tub. You can use the paper cup over there on the bed table if you want a drink of water. You missed dinner, so if you're hungry I can probably drum up a sandwich or broth or something. Just ask. If I can't get what you need, the worst thing that happens is I tell you no."

It all sounded way too friendly for what Tess was used to. Who was he? Where was she? What was going on?

It was obviously too late to get the answers to those questions now. She would need more information to get a handle on this situation. For now, she just wanted to be left alone.

"I think I'm fine. I can manage from here. Thanks."

"Okay, but if you change your mind or need anything, the nurses' station is just out the door and to your left."

Ah, the nurses' station. That was information Tess could understand. She was in a hospital of some kind for some reason. That helped a lot.

"Okay. Thanks. I'll come find you if I need anything. What was your name again?"

"Steve. I'm your nurse tonight. I'll be here until 7:30 tomorrow morning."

"Great. Thanks, Steve. G'night."

Steve left quietly, allowing light from the hallway in for just a moment as he left. Tess lay back on the pillow and fell asleep, contemplating what it all could mean.

So far her stay in the Looney Bin, as the patients so lovingly referred to it, was going well. She had been here a week. Lori and Gram had been to visit only two times and they were very nice and appropriately concerned. The doctors, and she used that word generously, had asked all kinds of very predictable questions. Tess had answered them with safe vagueness and been evasive enough to cause concern. Most of the information she planted was around risk for suicide. Tess held to the logic that if she were truly suicidal, she wouldn't tell anyone. Of course, if she played it too straight then they would release her and she wasn't ready for that. So, she played a bit of a mind game with them, employing responses that kept them guessing. It was working since the nurses, as well as Lori and Gram seemed careful not to antagonize her.

Tess was still not clear as to how she had gotten into this situation. It was apparent it was not Lori's idea. That was a good thing, since it meant that The Organization would have more limited control here since it did not appear to be their plan. Tess knew better than to overestimate them, however. They could very well have members within this environment. The shrinks or nurses, themselves, could easily be affiliated. That meant she needed to exercise caution in what she said while continuing to bait their minds. She had to admit, it was kind of fun.

Steve and Michelle were her two primary nurses. That meant most of the time it was one or the other of them assigned to her care. It wasn't like they had to come at every beck and call. By and large, the residents had full range of the floor to come and go as they

pleased. There were a few exceptions. When anyone lost it they would end up restrained and sedated, usually in their own rooms. Other times they were sent to solitary—a padded room with a heavy door and a window. That was a room that the residents were not permitted near. It was at the end of the hall, across from the janitor's closet. The next room up was the classroom that doubled as the library. After that there were several resident rooms, the Group room, the television room that was directly across from the nurses' station, then more resident rooms and the locked entry door. Behind the nurses' station were three offices, two of them belonging to shrinks and the third used as a conference or session room. Residents could go there to talk to their nurses or doctor. That was the extent of their world. They did leave the floor for Art Therapy and to go swimming, but those were earned privileges.

Most of the time it was pretty good here. She had located two suppliers to keep her system high enough not to experience withdrawal from the drugs, but she was careful to stay straight enough to pull off being functional. Since the first night of sedation, she had not had trouble with the hospital meds. That was important since she wasn't savvy enough to know what kinds of drugs wouldn't mix with her habit, just smart enough to know they might. She had steered pretty clear of that avenue. As long as she kept Nancy inside, all would be well.

Sometimes one of the other residents would start hallucinating, hollering or thrashing in one of the community areas or the hallway. It didn't take the orderlies and nurses long to sedate and control the situation and order was quickly restored. Occasionally, it would set off a chain reaction and several others would wack out, but overall, mayhem was short-lived. The only real danger that Tess considered was if the chaos triggered someone inside. It could get ugly that way. With the help of the Captains within, Tess worked the precarious balance.

It was worth the balancing act. This was far better than the world they came from. As far as Tess was concerned, she could stay here forever. Lori obviously had other plans. In the two hours she had

spent with Tess in the last week she had asked more than once, "What do you need to do to be able to come home with us?"

Tess' response was curt, "I don't know yet."

She wasn't sure how long that was going to be a satisfactory answer. For now, she was milking it for all it was worth!

Michelle came up to Tess and interrupted her thoughts. Tess had been sitting in a chair in the television room staring out the barred window, lost in her thoughts.

"What're you doing, Alissa?"

"Just thinking. No big deal."

"What were you thinking about?"

"Stuff."

"Any kind of stuff you want to share?"

"No, not really."

"Too bad. Group starts in ten minutes. I'm sure you'll be there, right?"

Group was mandatory. You didn't have to say a word, but you had to show up. "Yeah, I'll be down on time. Who's leading today?"

The facilitator for Group changed often. It depended who was on shift and who was qualified. "It'll be me today," Michelle stated.

"Cool. I'll definitely be there. I want to see how you handle us flakes!" Tess smiled.

"Flakes? There are no flakes here. You know that."

"Oh yeah, I forgot. We're all just on sabbatical from reality."

"Ha ha. Your words, not mine."

"Yeah, I know."

"Okay, well I'll see you in a few minutes. I have to go round up the rest of the masses."

"Good luck!"

Michelle waved back as she left the room. *Yeah*, Tess thought, *this was a much better life than anything I remember. I wonder how you get to stay on a permanent basis?*

She looked around. There was Ricky who, between the schizophrenia and the meds, lived in a whole different reality that Tess didn't even want to know about. Rob spent his hours in front of

the T.V., rocking forward and back, unreachable. Renee had convinced herself she was paralyzed from the waist down. The medical tests found no reason for the paralysis and there had been no injury. She just woke up with it one day. It had been long enough that the muscles in her legs had begun to atrophy and were pulled bent at the knees.

Tess decided maybe the price of becoming a permanent resident was a little higher than she cared for. After all, she couldn't go for a walk and listen to the trees and the birds. She really was trapped here, bars on the windows and a locked entry door. It was not pleasant when she thought about it. She heard the intercom announcement for Group and stood up. Maybe it was time to take some positive steps to getting out of here. She would think about it more later. She headed out the door.

"Steve, can I talk to you?"

Tess had decided to take a risk. She hadn't said a word in Group that afternoon but knew she needed to appear as if she were working to get herself out of here. Since she wasn't really sure why anyone thought she belonged here, she had to start somewhere. Steve was where she decided to start. Michelle was her first choice, but, having left shortly after Group, she was off for the next three days.

"Sure, Alissa. What do you need?"

"I was hoping we could talk."

"How about if we go into your room to talk? Rebecca is in with her doctor so your room's an empty space. Only one around here, I think."

"Yeah, that's fine."

They walked in. Tess flopped onto the bed and Steve pulled up a straight-backed chair.

"So, what's up?"

"Well, I wanted someone to be able to talk to. You're my nurse tonight, so I figure it should be you."

"Hey, that's a good start. What did you want to talk about?"

"First, I wondered if you could tell me how I got here. It's all a little

fuzzy and I can't seem to figure out exactly what happened. I was hoping you could make it a little clearer for me."

"I can tell you what I know. Apparently, you tried to jump through a plate of glass at home. Do you remember that?"

"No. Are you sure I didn't just fall through and maybe bump my head or something?"

"That's not the impression I got. You were placed here under a direct judge's order. That's pretty hard to do. There has to be some suspicious occurrence to have that happen. Have there been other instances you don't remember or strange things that happen that you don't understand?"

"Maybe. I guess the pressure at home just gets to me. It's not that bad, really, it just gets hard sometimes."

"What makes it so hard?"

"Well, my mom got divorced from my dad and he has visitation but, well, I don't think he really loves me. And I feel like she would rather have me with him. It wasn't until my grandmother asked my mom if I could stay home one weekend a month and go to church with her that I got to be at home on the weekends at all. So, I guess sometimes I just feel like no one really wants me. It makes me sad sometimes."

"I'll bet it does. What do you do when you get sad?"

"Pretend I'm not."

"Does that work?"

"Sometimes."

"Does it ever get overwhelming? Too much to just pretend it isn't there?"

"I guess. Maybe that's what happened the other day, with the glass."

"Maybe. What's life like at home, Alissa?"

"Difficult sometimes."

"Does anyone beat you or hurt you?"

That took Tess by surprise. It was more direct than she had ever heard before. She wondered why he was asking such a pointed question.

"No, why?"

"Well, you have some interesting injuries and scars. We have to do inventory when you arrive so we did it while you were sedated that first day. There were several questions raised."

Tess felt violated. Obviously Steve had not been the only one there. She calmed herself. It's not like it was the first time. Besides, they didn't hurt her, they just looked and it was in the name of medicine. She felt her anger wane.

"I live in a rough neighborhood. Inner city. We're a bunch o' tough little thugs!"

"I guess. Still, some of the things. Like that scar on your butt cheek."

"That's what happens when you're too slow in a knife fight, get it right in the ass. I was lucky that was all they got."

It sounded good. In actuality, Lenny had knifed her during an encounter gone bad, but she had to play it off. She didn't need anyone asking the wrong people the wrong questions. Nothing good would come of that.

"Hmmm. Not something I know much about."

"Yeah. I don't need anyone at home to beat up on me. Get plenty of that on the street and in school."

"I suppose. Like I said, I don't know much about that kind of thing. I was a suburban kid. Most violence we saw was the Baker kids across the street. They used to settle their sibling disputes with their fists."

"Multiply that by a trillion and you have my block," Tess smiled at Steve. He was a pansy after all.

"So, has anyone ever taken advantage of you?"

"Wha' d' you mean?"

"Have you ever been raped or sexually assaulted or molested."

Tess swallowed hard. Another direct question.

"Umm… I don't think I want to talk anymore."

"I'm sorry. I didn't mean to offend you. I just know that on the streets…"

"I said I'm done now."

Tess stood up and walked out of the room before Steve even got to his feet. It was a little more than she could handle. A little less direct she might have been able to talk her way through it. She knew she had blown it. Steve would have to be an idiot not to figure out that there was something more there. If there was one thing Tess was sure of, people made a lot out of everything here. Hell, if someone talked different one day from the next people raised their eyebrows, like that was unusual or something!

Tess heard the door open in her sleep. As she opened her eyes in the darkness, she saw a shadow standing over her. Before she could say a word, she felt the needle in her hip. As she slipped into the nothingness of sedation, she felt her nightshirt being lifted over her head and her panties being taken down. By the time she felt the weight on top of her, she was too far-gone to do anything about it.

Nancy screamed her way into the body. Tess had been sedated, not Nancy. Nancy fought for all she was worth. She kicked, bit, and screamed. The high pitch wail brought running feet. She felt herself lifted, hit in the hip with a hypodermic and carried. She didn't know where, she was out cold in mid-air.

Tess came to, remembering what she could, not sure if it was a dream or reality. Then she looked around. She was in Solitary, stark naked. It had not been a dream. But who?

The door opened and Steve and another male orderly walked in. "That was not pleasant. You kinda lost it last night when I came to check on you. Threw your clothes off and started screaming. We sedated you and brought you here to sleep it off."

Tess noticed that the other man was putting a piece of cardboard over the window of the door. Steve looked over his shoulder, also noting the cardboard.

"Now, let's get on with what we were trying to take care of last night. See, Bill and I think you are just another one of those inner city whores who wants to get it every chance you can. We're here to give it to you. Ah, ah. No one can hear you. These walls are sound proof.

If you behave, we won't have to sedate you and you can walk outta here. Otherwise, well, another round of sedation, who knows. Maybe Bill or I will need to be satisfied again by then. You see where I'm goin' with this?"

"Prick."

Bill smacked Tess across the mouth. It knocked her back, but didn't hurt. She had experienced worse from bigger. These were amateurs. At least that was her first impression. They didn't seem to have any link to The Organization. They would have made that clear by now. However, given the situation, she was at their mercy, once again, the victim.

"Just give us what we came for. Personally, I want you to suck my rocks off. I always like a good blowjob. Just kneel down and open wide. Bill, he wants to feel those tits again. By the way, when we did inventory that first day, we got to check your whole body. You got no secrets, ya little whore."

Tess fought back the rage. She hated the whole thing. When Steve was done, Bill had gotten himself pretty hard from feeling her up. He shoved her back, spread her legs and went for the gold. Tess worked hard to prevent another of The Troops from coming out. She knew if she lost control of the outside now, a lot of things would be compromised. She stayed grounded and let him finish. Both done, Steve turned her over, bare ass in the air. He smacked her with his hand. Nothing compared to what her father could deliver. It was more like a fly buzzing around after having had the experience of being attacked by a swarm of hornets – irritating, but not harmful.

"That is to remind you to keep your mouth shut. Remember we can make your stay here a living hell. All we need from you is an occasional servicing. And it's all just between us. Got it?"

She glared into his eyes, "Yes," she spit the word.

"Good. You can leave now."

"I don't have any clothes."

"Oh yeah," he smiled. "Didn't anyone tell you? When you get thrown into solitary you have to leave the way you came in. That's how you came in."

Tess glared at him, but refused to give him the satisfaction of any further reaction.

"I'm outta here." And she walked out. As she walked the hallway to her room, she didn't even try to cover herself. A few residents lowered their heads, one whistled. The nurses said nothing. Tess didn't care.

Chapter 23: Dead Boys Don't Float...

Keeping Steve and Bill happy was a small price to pay for the life Tess had here. They only bothered her about once a week. Besides it was straight sex; no sadism, no abuse, and simple threats to keep silent. Not that Tess would have told anyway.

She was beginning to think maybe she was just a perp magnet. They seemed to peg her from a mile away. She let go a sigh, coming back to the world at hand.

She, David, and Shawn had left the floor with Randy, one of the nurses, and were headed to the indoor pool. They had a chance to swim only once or twice a week. Things on the floor had to be pretty quiet for one of the nurses to be able to slip away to take them. That didn't happen with much regularity.

But tonight things had gone well. The small numbers in the swimming group tonight reflected those who had earned the privilege. This was David's first time. He was 12 and had only been on the floor about two weeks. He had catatonic episodes that no one could explain. Medically he was healthy as an ox. If there was nothing notably wrong physically then apparently there was something not right emotionally. So he found himself on the Unit.

Shawn was 14, like Tess. He had been on the floor the longest of the three of them, about three months. He had issues with destructive, blind rage. He was working hard to find better coping mechanisms. Today had been one of those good days for him.

Despite their individual issues, or maybe because of them, the three enjoyed each other's company. They had easily become friends. In the two months Tess had been around, she and Shawn had grown particularly close.

Arriving at the pool, it was obvious they would be the only patrons this evening. The lifeguard slipped into a back room, phone glued to his ear. Randy sat back in a deck chair, sports section in hand. The kids hit the water, exploding with the childhood energy pent up over days of quiet control. They laughed and splashed with a zeal they had little opportunity to express.

David was not as skilled a swimmer as the other two. He could not venture beyond the shallow end, even with the kickboard he clung to. Shawn and Tess split their time between the deep and shallow ends, trying to be inclusive with the younger child. It was difficult. They ultimately found themselves spending more and more time attempting to outdo each other on the diving board, leaving David to toodle around alone.

Tess had just pulled off a beautiful half-gainer that she finished with a perfect pike. She dove deep, toward the base of the slope that linked the shallow and deep water. Her eyes caught sight of a dark shape, lying on the bottom of the incline, not moving. Getting closer, she realized it was David.

Panic rose inside her. She attempted to grab the boy but did not have enough air in her lungs to get them both to the surface. Breaking the water, she gulped in air, screaming.

"Randy! David's underwater and he's in trouble! Help!"

"I can't swim! Where's the damn lifeguard?"

As he disappeared in search of the lifeguard, Tess dove back down. This time she was able to get her arms under David's. His limp body made it harder to swim upward. All she could do once both their heads were above the water was to tread water, trying to support the other child's head on her shoulder. As Shawn came to help, she noticed David was not breathing. His normally chocolate brown body was ashen gray.

As the lifeguard finally hit the water, Shawn and Tess had David

almost to the side. Quickly a flurry of activity brought medical personnel out from nowhere. Shivering, Tess retreated to the far corner of the deck and watched.

Their efforts seemed successful as they got David breathing, but he was still unresponsive. As they rolled him out, urgent shouts of life and death decisions could still be heard. Tess just stared. Suddenly, a big man in a white shirt and tie descended upon her.

"What happened?" he seemed to be yelling.

Tess just stared at him, unable to formulate a thought, let alone words. She fought Nancy off, refusing to allow the switch she knew would most certainly result in a loss of control.

"Excuse me, sir." It was Randy. He had Shawn under one arm, towel wrapped around his shoulders, obviously shaken.

"I'll take her back upstairs with me to 4C. If you need to speak with either of these children you'll have to have a release signed by their parents and their psychiatrist. I'm afraid I have to take them upstairs to ascertain what reaction they might have to this trauma. There, the staff can best support them. I would urge you to contact the correct channels so that there is no compromise in your investigation."

"Yes, of course. You're right. What was your name again?"

"My name is Randy. I'm one of the nurses up on 4C. What was your name?"

"My name is Theodore Wagner. I'm the Chief of Security here at the hospital."

"Nice to meet you, Theodore. I'll let the staff know to expect to hear from you and your office soon."

"Thanks." To the children, Theodore said, "Don't worry kids. Nothing about this is your fault. It'll be fine."

Tess thought about how interesting his words were. David was not fine. She knew that. She and Shawn were, well, she wasn't quite sure 'fine' was a fair description there either. She glanced at Shawn. He was staring at his feet. She wondered what was running through his head. Any distraction she could find would be a welcome one. That way she didn't have to think about what was running through hers.

The doctors had been able to revive David's body. He was breathing with the help of a machine. The brain scan indicated he had significant damage. No one knew how much until he woke up. IF he woke up. They were able to determine that he was underwater without oxygen for at least ten minutes. Tess had learned that after four minutes without oxygen, brain cells begin to die. That meant David had lost six minutes worth of brain cells. No one could tell her how much that actually worked out to be or what parts of the brain were most likely to have sustained the injury. The issue now presented to the family was whether they were willing to take him off of life support and see if he could breath on his own. The alternative was unpleasant.

It was not easy for Tess to get the information. There had been lots of questions directed at her and Shawn. They had been questioned separately and together, several times. Although it was clear they were not to blame it was just as clear there was a need for someone to bear the burden. Tess figured the lifeguard was probably personally responsible and the hospital guilty for having hired him. That didn't look so good for them. But it looked even worse for David and his family.

Michelle kept Tess and Shawn as informed as she could. She knew that closure for the two would be helpful, regardless of the outcome. Not knowing would be worse than having to accept the death or debilitation of their friend. These were already damaged kids who didn't need one more thing to deal with. Here, within the unit, she hoped the staff would be able to give the children the support and coping skills they needed.

So, she gathered as many details as she could. Because of David's stay on the floor as one of her charges, Michelle had direct contact with the family. That kept the information about his condition quite accurate. The hospital, on the other hand, was trying to resolve the issue and shove it under the proverbial rug as quickly as possible. Who could blame them? It's not like it looked good for the hospital to be responsible for taking a physically healthy child and turning him into a vegetable.

Tess had some trouble with nightmares. She felt responsible. If she had been paying more attention to David, if she hadn't left him alone for so long, if she had been better at including him in their games, if they had all stayed in the shallow end... The *ifs* ran on and on. Most of her experience with death in the past was obviously someone else's responsibility. The adults now were quite clear that neither Tess nor Shawn bore any level of the blame. But she couldn't help how she felt. The one time in her life when she finds a good thing, an existence not riddled with pain, fear and torture, and it gets tainted. It had to be about her. Isn't that what her father always told her?

"You'll never amount to anything good. This is where you belong. This is where you came from. The rest of the world will just hate you. There's no other place for you. Suck it up and take your rightful place. It's your destiny."

Her destiny. There was still that unknown drive within her, assuring her she truly was meant for greater things, that this life was temporary. But here in the hospital she had experienced a glimpse of the different. It still held its tribulations. But people like Steve and Bill were everywhere. They were still better than her father and his people. But now, with all that had happened with David, even this place had turned into a nightmare. Tess began to believe it was all about her, about her worthlessness. The Universe knew and set out to destroy all she touched. After all, she belonged to the Devil. It was time to go back home where she belonged, where she hurt the innocent only when forced. Where she knew the rules. Besides, she had found herself pregnant.

Chapter 24: Responsibility to Life...

It had to be Steve or Bill's baby. Near as she could figure she was about 6 weeks along. This would be her fifth pregnancy. Only one child had she carried beyond about three months. The rest were miscarriages. The other had been born two months early, dead. She feared for herself and the life within her.

It's not like it was something difficult for The Organization to deal with, they did it all the time. With sex their favorite activity, breeding was supported and kept plenty of ready victims and members around. It made them all very disposable. Tess just didn't know how disposable this child would be, if it made its way out of her.

Upon her discharge from the hospital two weeks after David's death, Tess was home and having some trouble adjusting to her old world. She had kept up academically with her classmates, but not socially. She was at a loss as to the current shifts and rifts of who was who on the street. That was a precarious place to be. She hooked up with her old friends and worked hard to come up to speed. But it wasn't that simple. She was going to have to reclaim her place, especially now with a label of being crazy. Of course, if she played it right, that could work in her favor.

She began exercising unpredictable behaviors. She growled at people she passed, just for the effect. One day at lunch, she 'lost it' and took on one of the biggest girls in the room for no apparent reason. She got herself kicked around a bit, but rumors began to put

her back in the 'those to beware of' category. She liked that. Few would cross a crazy bitch that was willing to throw down over nothing. It helped keep her survival a little more predictable out there.

Then there was home. By the first weekend, it was as if she had never been gone. She was quickly placed back into her role as victim/perpetrator. No one seemed to care about anything except her ability to carry on and behave appropriately. The Troops continued as a necessary mechanism, ensuring the survival in this familiar environment. Sometimes, when she escaped back to the Sacred Place, Tess wished for the days back on the floor where life was good.

No one had asked about the pregnancy. There was little sense in trying to hide it. As full term approached, there was some concern from Gram about healthcare. Lori didn't see much need. She took Tess to Marge and Dr. B. Both said all was going well. The most recent trip to Marge, she commented that it looked like there were two babies, twins. Perhaps there should have been more concern, but outside of Gram, no one really seemed to care.

One afternoon, Lori arrived home from work, walked up to Tess and stated, "We'll be putting your babies up for adoption. Your father is handling the details. You won't have to deal with anything. It'll be fine."

No conversation. No discussion. It was a moot point. Almost 15, Tess knew she had no legal ground to fight with, even if she had the resources, which she did not. So, that was how it would be.

The first pains of labor began about four o'clock one afternoon, while Tess was at softball practice. Familiar with pain, it felt more like pressure. Tess went into the girls' restroom and found blood down her leg. She knew this was not a good sign. She phoned Gram to come get her.

The older woman had already called Dr. B and was on her way. She left a message at Lori's office for her, telling her she was taking Alissa over to the hospital. She was pretty sure Lori would not be happy. She would have preferred to take Alissa to that woman across

town. Gram didn't know her, had never met her, but didn't like her. This was working out much better.

Alissa met her in front of the school, looking worried but in no apparent pain.

"Does it hurt much?"

"No. All I feel is a push in my muscles sometimes. Where we goin'?"

"I'm gonna take you over to County. Dr. B. has called ahead for us so they'll be waiting."

"What about Mom?"

"I left her a message. I'm sure she'll be along as soon as she can."

"Okay."

The rest of the twenty-minute trip was in silence. Gram marveled at how well her 14-year-old granddaughter was handling the trauma of labor and childbirth. It seemed she barely noticed.

Upon arrival at the ER entrance, an orderly met them with a wheelchair.

"Having a baby, are we?"

"Twins," Tess offered as she sat herself in the chair.

"Wow. You okay? I'll try to take it easy."

"I'm fine."

"Cool. Let's get you inside and get on with it. Ma'am, if you want to stop at the registration desk, I'll get the little lady settled in and you can come see her when you're done."

"Thank you, young man. I'm her grandmother. Her mother should be along shortly."

"Sounds great."

Tess was inside, gowned and hooked up to a monitor in no time at all. The contractions were coming pretty quickly and were apparently pretty intense. Tess didn't react to them at all, much to the nurses' amazement.

"Alissa, if you decide you need anything for pain, you let one of us know."

"Okay. Thanks."

Lori came in. "Your father is in the waiting room. He's contacted

the adopting parents. Everyone is ready."

It didn't seem to take too long before Tess was told to bare down and push. A couple of those and the doctor had her stop.

"We're gonna have to take these babies Cesarean, Alissa. You just don't seem to have what you need to bring them out this way and I don't want to risk any further delays. We're having trouble holding the heartbeat on the one baby. Let's not take any chances."

She was whisked off to the operating room. They administered an epidural, wanting her to be as aware as possible to reduce risk to her and the babies.

The first infant out made no noise. The rush of the nurses told Tess something was wrong.

"Is it a boy or a girl," she asked weakly.

"It's a boy. But he's not doing too well. Hang on, here comes his brother."

This one wailed from the moment he emerged. Tess smiled. She couldn't see him, but it was good to know he was pretty healthy.

"I'm sorry, honey. The first little guy didn't make it. Not sure what went wrong. But this second one, he looks real good. Do you want to see him?"

Tess knew she should say no. It wasn't her baby. She was giving him away. Not that she had a choice.

"Yes, please. Can I hold him for a minute?"

"Sure."

The nurse laid the slimy little one on her chest. He looked up at her and she felt the tears in her eyes.

"Hello, little one. You have a great life, okay? Bye, sweetie."

And she gave him back to the nurse.

"Can I hold the other one, please?"

"I'm sorry. They already took him out. It's probably better this way. I understand this little guy will be going to an adoptive home."

Tess sighed, "Yeah, I guess."

"I'm sure a few years from now you'll understand it as the best thing you could do for him. You're pretty young yourself. You got a lot of growing up to do before you're ready for that kind of responsibility."

Logical words from an adult who knew so little. Tess was sure she was right. Her life was hell for her. She didn't want the same for her baby. But suddenly, thoughts came together, hitting Tess with a new reality. Her father had arranged the adoption. Where did she think he was sending this baby? It's not like he was going to let it go outside of The Organization.

The reality stung her heart. She had an opportunity to have a positive influence on life and she had failed. Again. She slipped away to the Sacred Place.

Chapter 25: Reprieve??

Mig had been created by Alissa at the rite of passage at the age of 15. She had taken her place among The Troops as the Captain of the Intellects. This platoon of The Troops had the responsibility to keep life moving smoothly by simply keeping mind over matter, living in their heads. Mig was good at her job. She had no initial reactions; not to pain, fright, terror, tears, joy… nothing. She had the ability to step back, assess the situation and determine the most logical, least consequential reaction and provide it. All within a matter of seconds. She was calculated, good at reading the expectations of other people and great at denial. She spent a lot of time out in the body, having a high need for control.

She was also a great car thief. She knew that in the early years she had been taught to pick locks. That training had not ended. She now could open just about any lock on the market. The Organization soon recognized her skill and made good use of it lifting cars. Mig loved the thrill of popping a lock, hot-wiring the wheels and speeding away. The only thing that gave her a better high was the drugs that served as her reward.

The team had stayed the same over the years. It was her, J.R., Tammy and Johnny. Unlike before, they worked much more independently. In the past they had each had a job. Now they were all supposed to be able to do the entire job themselves. That meant they could be dropped in a parking lot or parking garage and each leave with a vehicle. Sometimes one needed a little help from another,

especially with some of the new-fangled locks. Mig was expected to make sure they all got into their respective cars. After that, she could finish her own work.

Each night on the job they were given specific choices. There was usually a list of which cars were acceptable. The list was not written down. It was given verbal. The first ones rattled off were the most desirable. Those were the ones Mig tried hardest to find. The better the payout, the better the stuff was you got paid and the longer you got to escape from reality.

They averaged twelve cars a week as a team. That was pretty good. J.R. didn't like their boss. Johnny liked to please J.R. Mig didn't much care and Tammy spent most of her time looking over her shoulder. Mig wasn't sure if Tammy's fear was actually that high or if her drug habit left her paranoid. It didn't matter. As long as they all came through, kept her payoff good, Mig could care less what they thought, felt or did.

Until the night they got back to the garage. It was too quiet. Something was terribly wrong. Mig and Tammy had gotten back a little behind the other two, Tammy's lock requiring a little more time which slowed Mig down.

They parked the cars around back behind the gate. Here the fence was lined. Walking around the front, Mig grabbed Tammy's arm and pulled her to the ground along the side of the garage near the trashcans.

"Thanks, boys. Took care of an old problem for me. You're payment is right where we agreed it'd be." J.R. hung up the phone on the wall and turned to Johnny. "We, my friend, are now the new leaders of this here operation. No one'll know any dif'rent." He laughed and Johnny joined him.

Mig kept a hold on Tammy, finger to her lips indicating silence. They slunk back to the cars. Mig slammed the door and had Tammy do the same. Then they walked back to the front of the garage, as if they had just gotten there.

"Oh, my god! Alissa, Tammy, it's awful. I dunno what happened! The place is all shot up! The boss and his crew. They're all dead! Whadda ya think happened?" It was Johnny, well-faked panic in his voice.

Tammy just stood there. Mig wasn't sure she had any idea what was going on.

"Well, we better call Dargon and tell him what's up. He ain't gonna be too happy, ya know. He liked the work outta this garage." Mig made sure her voice didn't give away the fact that she knew they were lying. It would cost her more than she wanted to pay. Survival was the name of the game.

"Yeah, I guess you're right." J.R. looked her dead in the eye, searching for any doubt, hoping to find fear. It was not Mig's way to let folks read her face. She stared back.

Ultimately, operations didn't change much, except now J.R. ran the racket. Mig wasn't sure what he was pulling, but she knew he was benefitting in more than one way. She let it go. All she wanted to do was survive. That was her job.

Almost 17, there was a light at the end of the tunnel. Alissa had withstood this life of perpetual abuse and pain. Because of who her father was, she was being primed to take her place as a leader among The Organization. There was nothing she wanted less. As her senior year began, she looked to the future and made plans to escape.

It's not like she was going to try to run off. She knew from experience that was an exercise in futility. She had a better idea. She was going to college. Of the seven cousins before her, only one had graduated from high school and none had gone on to college. She had identified college as her ticket out from under the life she knew. She had been planning it for years.

She had kept her grades at a solid 3.8 GPA. But her real trump card was music. Thinking back, she remembered when she was 8 years old, the night Grandpa had handed her a guitar.

"My back up guitar ain't comin' tonight. I need you to take this here thing and follow me."

And so she did. Where his fingers went on his guitar, she copied to hers. By the third song, she was doing great and loving it. It was her musical debut. After that, she played along with her grandfather, grandmother and uncle two or three times a month. By the time she

was 12, Grandpa would sometimes even let her take lead guitar on a song or two. She was a regular and the crowds loved the prodigy.

When she got to high school, she joined the band. Her musical talent quickly found her able to play multiple instruments. At the encouragement of her band director, she began to compete. By her junior year, she had made a name for herself across the state within the competitions. She ranked 9th in the state on tuba and 15th in the state on trombone. In between her sophomore and junior years, she had submitted an application for a music scholarship to one of the best schools in the nation. Her audition was in two months.

She had chosen trumpet as her instrument for college and the audition. Her band director had his reservations, but knew better than to stand in her way. He was not disappointed. She chose a moderately difficult piece and a good friend to accompany her on the piano. With practice, the duet was smooth and clean. It showed off her strengths of range and difficulty.

The other part of the audition would be sight reading. She had decided to do her sight reading on both the trumpet and the trombone. That would provide an example of her ability to read both clefs. Having spent the last three years on trombone and tuba, she was well versed on the bass clef. She wanted that to shine through in the audition. The last several months she had used to learn and master the trumpet, which used treble clef. She had also familiarized herself with the clarinet, alto sax and flute. She wasn't fluent, but she could play them. Add that to the guitar and piano she played with ease and her pretty good voice and she hoped it all added up well to a music scholarship.

Then, ten days before her audition, her father found himself in the middle of an ugly situation. He was being charged with a triple homicide. Mig was pretty sure the only way that kind of thing could have happened to him was if he pissed off the wrong people. That meant he was in a lot of trouble in more ways than she knew. The threat of doing time loomed over him. She tried hard to focus on her own affairs and let thoughts of what it might mean for her fall to the back of her mind.

It paid off. Her audition went magnificently. The only error in the whole duet had been the pianists. That wouldn't count against her. The questions the panel asked included how long she had been playing trumpet. There was an obvious awe when she explained she had only picked it up in the last three months. She continued to razzle and dazzle them with her skills on trombone and, at their request, sight reading on piano. Mig had felt a pang of fear when they asked her to sight read a piece to sing, but fortunately it was not that difficult and she was able to pull it off. She felt great when she left.

When she walked through the door at home her mother's face told her things here were different, far from good. Mig looked at her mother in anticipation, hoping the news was not something that would impact her plans.

"It looks like your father's gonna settle for a plea bargain. His lawyer says they could give him the death penalty. Life in prison's better. What're we gonna do?"

Mig didn't think it sounded so bad. With the man gone, maybe the abuse would stop. That would be a good thing. Didn't her mother understand that her abuse would stop, too? No matter how she looked at it, Mig couldn't see the bad news here.

"So, what does that mean for us?"

"Who knows…"

Her mother walked out of the room, as if she couldn't even see Mig anymore. Gram was sitting at the table, eyes fixed on Alissa.

"Whadda ya think, Gram?"

"Bad men belong behind bars. I dunno why she's so upset."

Mig and Gram were always on the same page. Mig smiled. Gram smiled back.

She was wrong. It could get worse. With Dargon out of the picture, the world went mad. There was a bloody battle over who would be the new leadership. In the end, Uncle John rose to the top.

Not that such a thing surprised Mig. The man was meaner than her father. She had watched him commit bloody atrocities, snuffing out life like it was worth nothing, then sit down to a plate full of steak

and baked potatoes. His eyes were cold, hollow. Not that Mig would ever be caught looking him in the eye. When he was looking at another she could see his eyes. If the eyes were the mirror to the soul, this man didn't have one.

Mig seemed to be Uncle John's personal project. He had tried hard for years to create within Alissa a blood-thirsty beast that could prey on the weak. Maybe he was trying to guarantee his own immortality by creating someone like himself. But no matter how hard he tried, she would not break.

As Dargon's daughter, it was illegal to kill her. She was fair game to rape, ravage and bring to the portal of death, but it was well known that the one who caused her to cross over that portal would withstand a fate worse than death.

But Dargon was gone now. Sort of. Uncle John had assumed the reigning role, but he had not been bestowed the title. There were interesting connotations in that fact. Dargon had been sent to the Pen for life. The Organization had enough links into the Pen to ensure his death or survival. Knowing their connections, Mig was sure Dargon had not gotten himself imprisoned without some significant error. But it was obviously a deed that warranted warning, not death. So, he had not been forced to relinquish his title. Did that mean that Alissa's survival was still a guarantee?

She had no way to be sure. One thing was sure. The abuse was not ending. As Mig continued to contrive and work her escape plan, the barrage on her mind, body and soul continued. The Troops guaranteed survival. They protected what was important. Mig just needed the energy and wherewithal to put the plan into motion. She feared if her escape to college did not work, Uncle John would eventually kill her and get away with it.

Chapter 26: Not What She Had Hoped...

Mig had managed the full academic and music scholarship. She was on her way to freedom. By the time her senior year ended, she was half packed and working on securing a job on campus, so she could move as soon as possible. She was out of the house with a car and all her earthly belongings by the end of July.

But it didn't play out the way she had hoped. She had thought she could just slip away, forgotten. Instead, she learned that The Organization was national, that the arms and legs of the beast spread everywhere. She had little opportunity to get out from under the watchful eye.

Thugs, making it perfectly clear where they were from, showed up everywhere. Her book bag turned up missing in the library to be found across campus under a tree with a note in it, "Don't forget where you belong."

Her campus mail was full of cryptic notes that bore warnings she would understand. Twice she had been caught alone on a dark walkway on campus and been raped, familiar words spoken to remind her that she was one of "them."

The message was clear. The Organization didn't want her to forget to whom she belonged. They wanted to prevent her from thinking she was better than they were, no longer a part of things or could succeed outside their world.

Mig remained cautious, fearful. It was not just the external

demons that plagued her. During the day, she could hold her own from the chaos within. But at night, she lost control. The fear and mayhem within The Troops took over. Nightmares consumed her sleep, switching from one personality to another. It was a revolving door with no one at the controls. Littles ran in and out, reliving their horror, screaming out in the middle of the night, bringing too much attention in their direction. The night terrors became dangerous as different personalities acted out the terrible deeds they had been forced to be a part of, sometimes fighting sleep demons so real they would lash out at those trying to help.

They had gotten so bad that Mig had requested and been granted a room of her own, unwilling to allow anyone else to run the risk of danger from the nightmares. She had already pounded on a cement wall to the point of having broken her own hand in three places. Additionally, one of her best friends had tried to calm her only to be met with a blow to the head that resulted in a concussion.

Mig would use drugs and caffeine to stay awake for days on end, fearing sleep. It took its toll on her studies and her health, but she had few alternatives. It got so bad one of her professors required her to seek help from the mental health professionals on campus. Mig was leery, but the prof had made it clear she would fail the class if she did not provide proof of her presence at appointments. There was little choice.

Mig liked the counselor immediately. Becky was not much bigger than Mig and had a friendly smile. Her office was filled with stuffed animals, pillows and soft couches and chairs. It felt safe.

Not that Mig was unfamiliar with the mental health field. Some of The Troops had spent time in a psych ward before Mig's arrival, but even after that, there were frequent referrals by the school and authorities. None of those had felt like this place though.

The first session, Becky laid out the rules, emphasizing the importance of having this as a safe place. Mig listened, softening to the idea of talking to this woman. It could be good.

"Alissa. Tell me about your nightmares. I have here in my notes from your personal file that you have had two psychotic episodes."

"What?" Mig knew nothing about such a thing.

"Well, it appears that on one occasion you woke up from a nightmare and behaved as a young child. A close friend of yours, Ellen, talked with you, convinced you that it was safe. When the Residential Aid for your dorm got there she was told you were convinced you were 7 years old and had to do something so your father wouldn't continue to hurt you."

Mig sat dumbfounded. How had she not known that one of the Littles had gotten out for such an extended time period? Thinking back, she realized she had experienced a lot of lost time. She had always assumed it was the result of the nightmares or the drugs and alcohol she still consumed. This new information was a little scary.

"The other incident you went through six hours with several people in the room with you. During that time you went from behaving like an infant and small child to what appeared to be re-enactments of being raped and beaten. More than once during that episode bruises were noted on your body that would then disappear. You talked some, relaying information and begging and pleading for things to stop."

Becky paused. Mig stared off, still dazed. She felt herself fading, shifting back to the Sacred Place.

"Can I p'ay wit' yer toys?"

Becky was a little confused. The comment was incongruous with what she was just discussing. She had watched Alissa's face remain stoic throughout her reiteration of the psychotic events at the beginning of the session. Becky thought she had recognized a glimpse of confusion, but was unsure. The voice she now heard, not the same one that she had heard a few moments before, was that of a small child. She suspected Alissa might be experiencing another psychotic episode. What had left this young woman so torn?

"Do you have any questions about what I've said so far?"

"Me not know. Jus' wanna p'ay. You say safe here, huh?"

"Yes, it's safe here."

"You want me do you or sumpin'?"

"Hmm. I'm not sure what you mean."

149

"If you not hurt me, you cin tuch me an' stuff. Den you let me p'ay yer toys, 'k?"

Becky understood the sexual context, obviously inappropriate sexual contact being used to bribe the use of the toys.

"I don't think that will be necessary. You can play with my toys anyway."

"Really?"

"Sure. What toys do you want to play with?"

"I like da bears. Cin I ho'd 'em?"

"Sure. While you're holding them, can you close your eyes for me and tell me what you see?"

"No."

"No? Why not?"

"Don' see nuffin wit' you eyes closed. Hee hee."

"You're right. Well, here are the bears. What do you think?"

"I t'ink dey's sof'. I like sof'."

"Yeah, me too."

Becky wasn't too sure what she was supposed to do now. This was a new experience for her. She *was* sure she could not let Alissa leave her office until things were under better control. Becky wasn't sure how to do that just yet.

She was familiar with inner child work and regression, but this was a little different than she had seen before. Normally the work was therapist driven with the client seldom losing awareness. Becky didn't think there was much control in this situation.

Obviously there was trauma in Alissa's life. It was just going to take some time to figure out what it was and how to help her get a better grasp on reality. For now, Becky entertained the apparent young child in her office.

After about twenty minutes, the child turned to her and announced, "A'done now. Bye" And she was gone. In her place, Becky had a sleeping young woman. She wasn't sure what to expect or what to do, so she did nothing. A few moments later, Alissa stirred.

"Hey, how're you feeling?"

"Who're you?"

Tess didn't know where she was or what was going on. She had been around some for the college experience, mostly the drunken weekends and a little of the psychology class she enjoyed. But this was a different place, some place she hadn't been before. The woman sitting in front of her was unfamiliar.

Becky was flying by the seat of her pants, "My name is Becky. You came here today to talk with me. Do you remember?"

Tess had been a part of The Troops long enough to know how to play this game.

"Oh, yeah. I was just confused for a minute."

"I can understand that. Do you remember anything about what we've been doing here today?"

Tess looked around. Bears sat beside her on the couch. Becky sat across from her with a pad of paper and a pen. Some kind of shrink, Tess was sure.

"Yeah. But I'm kinda tired now. Can we set something up for another day?"

"Are you sure you're ready to leave? I want to know that you'll be safe when you leave here."

"I'm fine. Just tired. I'll go back to my room and hang out for a little while. No problem."

"Okay, but I'd like you to come back tomorrow about 2. Do you have a class?"

"I don't think so, but let me check. If I don't call you, I'll be here. Okay?"

"Sounds good. Here's the paper you need for Professor Wagner. I'll see you tomorrow."

"Okay. Thanks."

Tess left the building and had to reorient herself to the campus. She had not been in this building before. Slowly, she identified where she was and began walking to the Student Union to get her mail. She mused about what might have happened since she was last out. What day was it? Sometimes this was a little harder than she cared for. Just another day, she guessed.

Getting her mail, she stopped short when she saw the return

address on the envelope in her hand. It was the penitentiary that held her father. He had written her a letter. She didn't know if that made her afraid or happy. She decided it was probably better to wait and read it when she was alone. Placing the envelope at the bottom of the stack, she left the Student Union and headed for her room, curiosity getting a better grip every step of the way.

Finally in her room, she opened the envelope. It was written on plain lined notebook paper. The spelling was poor and the grammar not great, but it was legible.

Dear Alissa;

I hope you doing good in school. I dint tell u how prowd I am a you. You is a smart girl. I know u doin' good. I wan tell you how sorry I am. I been a lowsy dad all your life and wan try be better to u and your mom. I mite get out here soon and then you an me coud start over agan have a good rlatinship. I won hurt you no more. I wan stop drinkin and thos bad things so I can be a good daddy for you. I call you wen I no wen I getn out an you can com to see me. That be good. We have us a new relshonship. I alwas love u. Now I gon show you. You can rite me if you wan. I wud like that a lot.

Love,
Your daddy.

Tess let the paper hit the floor. She didn't know what to think. It had been a trying day. She thought about the things her father was responsible for in her life. None of it was good. Feeling overwhelmed, Tess closed her eyes, tight, and went to the Sacred Place.

Mig sat on the bed, a letter on the floor at her feet. She read it, wondered how long she had been sitting there. She couldn't figure

out why her father would write such a letter. Within her, voices raised in hopes it was the daddy they had all longed for, the one who could love them and treat them as their father and not like the Devil. Mig wasn't so sure.

Last thing she remembered she had been with Becky. Mig wasn't sure how that had turned out. She rummaged through the stack of mail and found the appointment slip for tomorrow with Becky. Two o'clock. That would work.

Her head hurt. She decided she would lay back for a minute then get ready and hit the bar. Tying one on sounded like a great solution right now.

Chapter 27: Healing Opportunities...

Mig was back in Becky's office. She knew that it was foolish to continue to deny the abuse in her life. She also was pretty sure she didn't want to get into any trouble with anyone, not at home nor here. She had to figure out how to walk the fine line. The rules forbid her to tell. But this woman already knew that Alissa had been physically and sexually abused. Mig figured she would just provide a partial picture. If they were ever to truly get out from under the thumb of The Organization, someone was going to have to know something. Might as well start the tightrope walk now.

"So, where are we going to start today, Alissa?"

"Where do you want to start?"

"Let's try where we started yesterday. Tell me about the nightmares."

"I don't usually remember them."

"Usually. What do you remember?"

"It's about my dad."

"What about your dad?"

"Well, he used to come and do stuff to me. If I didn't behave he would whip me with a belt. Sometimes he would hit me with his hands."

"What kind of stuff did he do?"

"You know, stuff."

"No, I don't know. Can you tell me?"

Mig sat silently, unable to find the words. She was already sweating. What she had already said could get her killed. But at the same time, the terror had a companion emotion within her. It was relief. It felt good to tell someone.

"No, not really."

"You talk about your father in the past tense. Why is that?"

"He's been in prison for almost two years."

"What was the charge?"

"He killed three guys in a bar fight. I don't know much more. I got a letter from him yesterday. That's kinda weird and I think it bothers me a little."

"Bothers you how?"

"He talks about wanting to have a wonderful relationship with me, when he gets out. But he's supposed to be in for life."

"So, what if he wanted to try again, had turned over a new leaf. Would you be willing to try?"

"I don't know. He hurt me a lot. But I really would like a real father for a change. But can people really change like that?"

"I think they can, with the right motivation. When was the last time he hurt you?"

"Shortly before he went to the Pen."

"So it hasn't been that long. You don't have any real reason to think he's really so much better, huh?"

"I guess not. But maybe..."

"Let's get back to the nightmares and the psychotic episodes. Do you remember anything about what happened at our session yesterday?"

"Some."

"Do you remember playing with the bears with me?"

"Maybe."

"How old were you pretending to be?"

Mig didn't like that question. She didn't know how to answer it. She looked at Becky. This was not going too well, by her definition.

"I'm not sure I understand the question. I don't think I want to talk about it anymore."

Afraid of what she might trigger by not honoring the request, Becky backed off.

"Okay. What do you want to talk about?"

"I want to figure out how to make it all go away so I can get on with my life. It's in the past. Now I just want to be me."

"I can understand that, but you're going to have to talk about the things that happened so you can let them go. Maybe it would be easier if you wrote them down. Can you journal?"

Many within The Troops had journaled over the years. Most of it was nothing anyone could make sense of. There were a few pieces of poetry that were pretty good. That was about it. Mig had never tried writing things down. It seemed a little too frightening. If telling was bad, writing things down had to be worse. Or maybe not. Formally there had been no "telling" if you wrote it down. It might be read which was still "reading" not "telling." Well, that was a mind game that might work.

"I can try."

"Good. Why don't you see what you can do and bring it in next week. Okay?"

"Okay."

They set an appointment for the next week and Mig headed over to the campus bookstore. They had some pretty neat writing books. Mig figured that would be a good way to start. She chose a soft-back, lined book with bears on the outside. It just seemed appropriate. Heading back to her room, the feel of the book in her hand seemed strengthening.

The Journaling was going well. Mig was not the only one who enjoyed it. Other personalities took turns writing their thoughts and feelings. Mig was always careful to choose what she shared with Becky, usually making a copy for her to read, not wanting to hand over the precious journal. There were some pretty dramatic entries. Besides, the handwriting changed almost by the page. Mig didn't need anyone asking questions about that, least of all Becky. The concept of psychotic episodes had not come up recently and Mig was

happy to allow it to be all but forgotten. She didn't know how to explain it and didn't want that kind of responsibility.

Becky was thrilled with the progress Alissa was making. The journal entries she had shared helped to explain some of the observations noted in her personal file. Alissa had withstood significant abuse that included breaks and bruises. The incestuous relationship with her father had been expanded to several of his brothers. Overall, Alissa seemed pretty together considering what she had experienced. They had not had any further discussions about the psychotic episodes. Becky felt confident that was something that could wait. As long as Alissa kept confiding in her, Becky was pretty confident the events would be less likely to reoccur.

Today the discussion took a new turn.

"Your father called the dorm?"

"Yeah. He's been out for about three weeks. Mom told him I have spring break coming up and he wants to see me."

"How do you feel about that?"

"Afraid. But maybe it would be a good thing."

"How so?"

"Maybe this shock probation is because he's figured out what an ass he was and wants to change it. Maybe he's found religion. I don't know. I just feel like maybe I need to find out."

"So you're considering meeting him?"

"Well, I guess."

"Alissa, promise me you won't go alone. You need to take someone with you to keep yourself safe."

"Okay, if I can. I don't know when I'll see him."

"Break starts this Friday. Can we squeeze in another session before then so you can tell me what your plans are?"

"I don't think so. I have three big exams this week and this has been a tough grading period for me, I can't afford to do poorly."

"I understand. Leave me a note on Thursday then, okay? Let me know what you decided."

"Okay. I'll try."

Chapter 28: Abrupt Changes...

Becky did not get a note from Alissa on Thursday. There was little she could do about it. She had to hope and pray that the young woman made the right decisions, that she had come far enough to know how to protect herself. Her thoughts filled with doubt. She whispered a prayer.

Spring break was hectic. There were lots of people Mig and Tess and Eris and others wanted to see. This was one of those times when one body holding so many was a detriment. They had to share their time. Some of it overlapped, people and places. Some did not. Every day was full of reconnecting with her old world. Much had not changed. But she had.

Mig found that home didn't feel the same anymore. She worked hard to avoid her mom, afraid of what or where she would be told to go. Gram was happy to see Alissa and cooked huge meals, noting that the child had lost weight in her time away.

Quickly, it was Sunday afternoon. Mig's plane would leave to take her back to school at 6 PM. A phone call that morning stopped her short.

"Hey there! How's ma girl? You gonna come see me today?"

It was her father's voice. She choked on any words, remembering the warnings Becky had given her. Regaining herself, she decided putting him off was the wrong thing to do.

"Hi, Dad. Sure. I can swing by your place about eleven this morning. Gotta make my plane by this afternoon."

"Sounds great. I'll be waitin'."

Very strange conversation. But it was over. She had just enough time to run down the road and say her farewells to Danny and his family and head out to her father. She left a note for her mom, assuring her she would be back by 4:00 so they could leave for the airport.

Her time with Danny had been short. Now she was on the road out to her dad's house. Becky was going to kill her. Not only had she agreed to meet him, but she was going to his house and she was going alone. Deep inside she knew it was not her best decision. But, also deep within, she prayed for a loving father who could give her what she had never had—a daddy.

Pulling up in front of the house, she was relieved to see another car. There was someone else here. She walked up the walkway. She put her hand into her jacket pocket and felt the switchblade there. She took comfort, hoping she wouldn't need it.

She knocked on the door and he came and answered it. They sat in the living room and chit chatted for a few moments. Bob, a friend of her father's, was there as well. Mig tried to determine if that was a comforting thought or not. Within those few moments, her father had moved to the couch next to her.

Standing to move to the chair on the other side of the room, he grabbed her left arm, pulling her to the couch. Mig reached for the switchblade with her right hand, not yet opening it. He put his hand on her thigh and she clicked it open. It was the invitation he was waiting for.

"I missed you, my little whore. Long time without you. Always were my fav'rite. Now whadda ya doin' with that?" He motioned toward the blade.

"Leave me alone or I'll use it." Mig wondered where she got the balls to say that to him.

"Really?"

Bob was on his feet with a small caliber handgun pointed at her. "I'd think twice, perty," he sneered.

159

Mig started to stand while swinging the blade at her father, more for show than with intent to hurt him. In one swift move he shoved her down, the back of her head hitting the heavy coffee table on the way down. Mig felt her world go dark.

When she came to, her head was spinning and it hurt like she had never known before. She was spread eagle and naked on the floor, hands tied to a couch leg over her head. She felt the familiar feeling of just having been raped and looked around, trying to orient herself. She was having trouble focusing her eyes. Her body felt like lead and it took more effort than usual to get her legs to move.

"Finally awake, huh, bitch? You missed the party!"

Her father was sitting on the chair, looking straight up at her from between her spread legs. She worked to close them, having to think hard to make them cooperate.

"I... a plane..."

Those were the only words Mig could get out of her mouth.

"Oh yeah. Can't have ya late fer school, now can we? Cut her lose, Bob."

Her hands were cut free, though she never saw Bob. She had to think her hands down, rubbing the wrists that had burns around them from the nylon cord they had used to tie her. As she tried to stand she became dizzy and fell to the floor. She looked around for her clothes. From somewhere, they were thrown at her.

They talked, but she couldn't understand them. She focused on dressing herself and ascertaining the damage. The only obvious mark was a cut near the outside corner of her right eye. It bled pretty profusely. She wiped the blood off her face with her shirt sleeve, steadying herself to stand. She walked to the door, hearing their laughter behind her. She didn't look back. It was all she could do to walk to the car.

It was 3 something. She still couldn't see real well. She had to hurry to get home so her mom could take her to the airport. She got lost a couple times. It was a trip she had made a thousand times, but she kept turning down the wrong streets. Once on the highway, she missed her exit and had to turn around. Finally, she parked the car in

front of her house. Her mom was waiting impatiently by the door. Mig took a deep breath and sauntered out of the car, trying to look cool, not nauseous like she felt.

"What happened to you? You're twenty minutes late. We gotta get you to the airport so you get outta here on time. I got yer bags in the car a'ready. Get in there. What happened to your eye?"

"Tripped. Hit the door. It's fine." Mig hoped the words weren't as slurred as they felt. Of course, she was an addict. Her mom probably wouldn't notice anything out of the ordinary even if the words were slurred.

Her mom raced to the airport. Mig worked hard to keep her eyes open all the way, fighting the urge to drift to sleep. Her head was pounding. It was everything she could do to keep from throwing up. When she got out at the airport, she lost the battle. The bile and stomach contents spewed out. The action made her even more woozy and she had to lean on her mom to walk.

"You a'right?" Her mom sounded genuinely concerned.

"Yeah. Fine." Mig just wanted to get on that plane and get out of here.

She boarded the plane slowly, using the sides of the gangway to steady herself. She had a two-hour flight to Chicago where she had to catch a second plane to get her safely to school. It was going to be a long two hours.

Mig had gotten a couple aspirin from one of the stewardesses and sipped on a ginger ale. She floated in and out of consciousness, working hard not to totally lose it. As they circled Chicago the pilot announced that there was a huge delay due to another plane having run off the runway. Mig groaned. She wasn't sure how much longer she could hold out.

The minutes ticked into hours. Finally, having spent more time circling the airport than it had taken to get there, they landed. The next announcement told the passengers with connecting flights that all the planes had already left the airport. They were told to check the courtesy gate to determine when their next flight would leave. Mig

asked a stewardess for a wheelchair, telling her she wasn't feeling well enough to walk.

The stewardess found a chair and helped Mig exit the plane. At the courtesy counter, she was told her next flight would not leave until 6:30 the next morning. The airline was planning to put her up for the night in the Airway Hotel and would, of course, provide her with a voucher for dinner from room service. Another place, another time, it would have sounded great. Tonight, the news made Mig groan.

Once in her room, she called Ellen. She mumbled a semi-coherent account of what had happened, explaining to her friend that she didn't think she was going to make it through the night. Ellen talked with her all night. She assured Mig that everything would be just fine. She would call the airline and let them know that Mig was critically injured and see what she could do. As they hung up, Mig wasn't sure she would ever really see her friend again. Everything was dark and fuzzy.

At five thirty, there was a knock on the hotel room door. Mig couldn't get up to answer it. She tried to vocalize a welcome. Nothing came out. All she could do was lay on the bed and stare at the fuzzy ceiling.

People entered. Mig was lifted and placed in a wheelchair. She almost felt relief as the world went black. Nothingness was a welcome friend.

Tess had an awareness of people around her, medical people. Someone was in her face, but she couldn't hear them, could barely see them. It was all happening around her, to her, like she wasn't even there. Her eyes couldn't focus. She couldn't move her arms or legs. Breathing was difficult. Then darkness.

"We can't fully assess the extent of the injuries. Right now she has paralysis from the neck down, though there is more sensation on the right side of her body then the left. We won't know the extent of the impact on the processing centers of the brain until she regains

consciousness. Right now we have her heavily sedated as we wait for the swelling in the brain to go down and seizure activity to decrease. It's the swelling that has caused most of the injury. If she had gotten medical attention sooner, the injury would have been significantly less severe." The doctor spoke into the phone. The mother on the other end, several states away, seemed at a loss as to what to say or do. He paused, listening.

"Ma'am, she's not stable enough to even consider moving at this time. If you want to come down and see her while we wait for her to stabilize, that might be the most productive thing you can do. It's a waiting game from here." Again he paused, waiting. His own thoughts clearly outlined that he would not release this patient for transfer until a clear explanation of how she had come to be in this bad a condition was obtained.

"We have an idea that someone did this to her. She was not able to communicate clearly to us in the trauma room. The injuries are indicative that they were inflicted. No one noted a fall or accident. We're going on the assumption this young woman was brutally beaten. Some of the non life-threatening injuries are congruent with a severe beating; broken ribs, bruises, contusions, etc. We may never know for sure. It will depend on her faculties when she regains consciousness. We'll bring her out of sedation slowly once the swelling goes down, probably within three to seven days. That's really all I can tell you. The prognosis is not clear. A lot of it depends on her."

In the Sacred Place, The Troops meandered, unneeded. There was a peripheral knowledge that things were precarious, but the promise of survival still held strong. If you listened closely, you could hear the drums of The Tribe Within The Troops. They grew louder, reminding anyone willing to listen that Truth still abided here, that the Red runs deep. The Ancients had bestowed a gift, not yet accessed. This was a child born to great things. The path of healing had begun. The journey of recovery would involve a reclaiming of, not just what was stolen from the body, but what was stolen from the

soul. The Spirit, however, well protected, lived on strong and whole. It was just a matter of time before all would come together and Laughing Star would remember her power, reclaim her place and lead where others dared not tread. She was an Indian whose path included the Red Road. She lived it, even now, without consciousness. Her choices were determined by it. Her real mother, Flower Beneath the Stone, had planted the seeds and they had taken root. Blooming would be slow, but beautiful.

The body slept peacefully, a drug induced sleep. For now, no one was home, the body vacant. A gathering of strength would be necessary. The battles would be great, but the victory guaranteed. After all, the Red runs deep and she was not alone.

Find out how Alissa's journey continues in *Making it Red.*

Printed in the United States
41542LVS00009B/45

9 781413 758955